Alan Wright, George Edward Farrow

The Wallypug in London

Alan Wright, George Edward Farrow

The Wallypug in London

ISBN/EAN: 9783743313378

Manufactured in Europe, USA, Canada, Australia, Japa

Cover: Foto ©ninafisch / pixelio.de

Manufactured and distributed by brebook publishing software (www.brebook.com)

Alan Wright, George Edward Farrow

The Wallypug in London

THE
WALLYPUG IN LONDON

BY

G. E. FARROW

AUTHOR OF "THE WALLYPUG OF WHY," "THE MISSING PRINCE," ETC

ILLUSTRATED BY ALAN WRIGHT

METHUEN & CO.
36 ESSEX STREET, W.C.
LONDON
1898

Chant Royal

ADDRESSED TO

HER MOST GRACIOUS MAJESTY QUEEN VICTORIA

IN COMMEMORATION OF 22ND JUNE, 1897

VICTORIA! by grace of God our Queen,
    To thee thy children truest homage pay.
Thy children! ay, for Mother thou hast been,
    And by a mother's love thou holdest sway.
Thy greatest empire is thy Nation's heart,
And thou hast chosen this the better part.
    Behold, an off'ring meet thy people bring;
    Hark! to the mighty world-sound gathering
From shore to shore, and echoing o'er the sea,
    Attend! ye Nations while our paeans ring—
Victoria's children sing her Jubilee.

The grandest sight the world hath ever seen
    Thy kingdom offers. Clothed in fair array,
The Majesty of Love and Peace serene,
    While hosts unnumbered loyalty display,
Striving to show, by every loving art,
The day for them can have no counterpart.
    Lo! sixty years of joy and sorrowing
    For Queen and People, either borrowing
From other sympathy, in woe or glee,
    Hath knit their hearts to thine, wherefore they sing—
Victoria's children sing her Jubilee.

With royal dignity and gracious mien
    Thine high position thou hast graced alway;
No cloud of discord e'er hath come between
    Thy nation and thyself; the fierce white ray
That beats upon thy throne bids hence depart
The faintest slander calumny can dart.
    Thy fame is dear alike to churl and king,
    And highest honour lies in honouring
The Sovereign to whom we bend the knee;
    "God save the Queen," one strain unvarying—
Victoria's children sing her Jubilee.

What prophet, or what seer, with vision keen,
    Reading the message of a far-off day,
The wonders of thy reign could have foreseen,
    Or known the story that shall last for aye?
A page that History shall set apart;
Peace and Prosperity in port and mart,
    Honour abroad, and on resistless wing
    A steady progress ever-conquering.
Thy glorious reign, our glorious theme shall be,
    And gratitude in every heart upspring—
Victoria's children sing her Jubilee.

Behold, ye tyrants, and a lesson glean
    How subjects may be governed. Lo! the way
A Woman teaches who doth ne'er demean
    Her office high. Hark! how her people pray
For blessings on the head that doth impart
So wise a rule. For them no wrongs do smart,
    No cruelties oppress, no insults sting,
    Nor does a despot hand exaction wring;
Though governed, Britain's subjects still are free.
    Gaze then—ye unwise rulers wondering—
Victoria's children sing her Jubilee.

ENVOY.

Queen Mother, love of thee doth ever spring
Within thy children's hearts, a priceless thing,
    Nor pomp nor state that falleth unto thee
Can ever rival this grand carolling—
    Victoria's children sing her Jubilee.

G. E. FARROW.

PREFACE

My dear little Friends,

You will no doubt be surprised to find this book commencing with a perfectly serious poem, and one which probably some of you will find a little difficulty in understanding. When you have grown older, however, and happen to look at this little book again, you will be glad to be reminded of the historic event which the poem commemorates. Now, about ourselves, when I asked in my last book, *The Missing Prince*, for letters from my little readers, I had no idea that I had so many young friends, and I can hardly tell you how delighted I have been at receiving such a number of kind letters from all parts of the world.

I do hope that I have answered everyone, but really there have been so many, and if by mistake any should have been overlooked, I hope my little correspondents will write again and give me an opportunity of repairing the omission.

Such charming little letters, and all, I am happy to find, really written by the children themselves, which makes them doubly valuable to me.

And how funny and amusing some of them were to be sure! And what capital stories some of you have told me about your pets.

Some pathetic incidents too; as, for instance, that of 'Shellyback,' the tortoise, whose little owner wrote a few months after her first letter to say that poor 'Shellyback' was dead.

I have been very happy to notice how fond you all seem of your pets, for I have always found that children who make friends with animals invariably have kind and good hearts. And the poor dumb creatures themselves are always so ready to respond to any little act of kindness, and are so grateful and affectionate, that I am sure it adds greatly to one's happiness in life to interest oneself in them.

PREFACE

One of my correspondents, aged eight, has embarrassed me very much indeed by suggesting that I should " wait for her till she grows up," as she should " so like to marry a gentleman who told stories." I hope she didn't mean that I did anything so disgraceful; and besides, as it would take nearly twenty-five years for her to catch up to me, she *might* change her mind in that time, and then what would become of me.

Some of my letters from abroad have been very interesting. One dear little girl at Darjeeling, in India, wrote a very nice descriptive letter, and concluded by asking me to write " something about the stars," and speaking of new stories brings me to another subject that I wish to talk to you about.

You know that I spoke in my last book about writing a school story, and one about animals. Well, when I found that so many of you wanted to hear " more about the Wallypug," I was obliged to put these two books aside in order to gratify your wishes. I hope that you will be as interested in hearing about his Majesty this time as you were last.

You will be sure to notice that the pictures

are by another artist, but Mr. Harry Furniss has been away from England for some months, and so it has been impossible for him to illustrate this volume. Some other time, perhaps, Dorothy and he will give us more of their work; but in the meantime Mr. Alan Wright has been very interested in drawing pictures for this book, and I hope you will be pleased with his efforts.

Now, about writing to me next time. When I asked you to address me under care of my publishers, I did not realize that in the course of business I might find it necessary to change them sometimes, and so to avoid any possibility of confusion, will you please in future address all letters to

 Mr. G. E. Farrow,
  c/o Messrs. A. P. Watt & Son,
   Hastings House,
    Norfolk Street, Strand.

What am I to do with all the beautiful Christmas and New Year's cards which I have received? Will you be vexed if, after having enjoyed receiving them as I have done so much, I give them to the poor little children at the hospitals to make scrap books with?

I happen to know how much they value and appreciate gifts of this kind, and by allowing me to bestow them in this way, your pretty presents will be giving a double happiness.

Well, I must conclude this rather long letter now, or I shall be accused of being tedious; but really it gives me almost as much pleasure to write to you, as it does to receive your letters. Good-bye. Don't forget that many of you have promised to write to me again, and that I am always more than glad to welcome any new friends.

Believe me, dear Children,
    Yours affectionately,
        G. E. FARROW

CHAPTER I

HIS MAJESTY AND SUITE ARRIVE

PIERROT

A MOST extraordinary thing has happened; the Wallypug has been to London! But there, I am forgetting that possibly you have never read *The Wallypug of Why*, in which case you will, of course, know nothing about his Majesty, and so I had better explain to you who, and what, he is.

To begin with, then, he is a kind of king of a place called Why, which adjoins the mysterious kingdom of Zum. I am afraid, though, that if you searched your atlases for a very long while you might not find either of these places, for the geographers are so undecided as to their exact position that they have not shown them on the maps at all. Some little friends of mine, named Girlie and Boy, have been there, however, and I can tell you, if you like, the way they went. This is the way to Why:

> Just go to bed and shut your eyes
> And count one hundred, one by one;
> Perhaps you'll find to your surprise
> That you're at Why when this is done.

I say *perhaps*, because this only happens when you have been particularly good all day, and *sometimes* boys and girls are not quite as good as they—but there, I won't say what I was going to, for I am quite sure that it would not apply to you. This is the way to Zum:

> Not when the moon is at its full,
> But just a tiny boat-shaped thing,
> You *may* see Pierrot sitting there
> And hear the little fellow sing.
> If so, just call him, and he'll come
> And carry you away to Zum.

There, now, I've told you the way to go to both places, so that, if you wish to, you can go there whenever you please.

HIS MAJESTY AND SUITE ARRIVE

I am telling you all this because one day in the spring Girlie and Boy, who live in another part of London, came to see me, and we had been talking about these things for about the hundredth time, I should think: for these children are never tired of telling me of all the strange things which happened to them when they journey to these wonderful places. In fact they were just arguing as to which was the most interesting place to go to, Why or Zum, when my housekeeper, Mrs. Putchy, came to the door with the unwelcome news that the carriage had come for my little friends, and that it was time to say good-bye. After they had gone I sat staring into the fire wondering where Why could be, and if there was really such a person as the Wallypug, when my little dog Dick, who had been lying on the rug before the fire, suddenly jumped up, and barking excitedly, ran to the other end of the study, where a picture, which I had bought the day before at an auction sale, stood leaning against the wall. Now this picture had been sold very cheap, because no one could tell at all what it was about, it was so old and dusty, and the colours were so dark and indistinct.

I had bought it hoping that it might prove valuable, and there it stood till it could be sent to be cleaned and restored. Imagine my surprise then, when, on following Dick across the study, I discovered that the colours in the

WITH SLIPPERS ON HIS TAIL

picture had all become bright, and were working one into the other in the most remarkable way, red running into green, and blue into yellow, while a little patch of black in the centre of the picture was whirling round and round in quite a distracting manner. What could it all mean? I stared and wondered, till, out of the confusion, there gradually grew shapes which bore some resemblance to human beings, and, presently, I could recognize quite distinctly, first a young man in knee breeches, smiling in a particularly self-satisfied way, and escorting a large fish, who was walking upright, with slippers on his tail, and who wore a waistcoat and necktie. Then an amiable-looking old gentleman, carrying a wand, who was followed by a curious little person, wearing a crown and carrying an orb and sceptre. A particularly stiff and wooden-looking soldier stood at the back of this strange group. Judge of my amazement when, quite as a matter of course, the whole party deliberately stepped out of the picture into the room, and, before I could realize what had happened, the old gentleman with the wand came forward with a flourish and an elaborate bow, and announced:

"A-hem! his Majesty the Wallypug of Why and suite."

I was so astonished that for the moment I could not think what to say, but at last I managed to stammer, as I made a low bow to the Wallypug:

"I am delighted to make your Majesty's acquaintance."

The Wallypug smiled very affably, and held out his hand.

"I have come up for the Jubilee, you know," he said.

"*We've* come up, you mean to say, Wallypug," corrected the old gentleman with the wand, frowning somewhat severely. "I am the Wallypug's professional adviser," he continued. "I am called the Doctor-in-Law—allow me to introduce the rest of our party. This," he went on, bringing the young man with the self-satisfied smile forward, "is the Jubilee Rhymester from Zum; he hopes to become a minor poet in time. And this, indicating the wooden-looking soldier, "is Sergeant One-and-Nine, also from Zum." Here the Doctor-in-Law took me aside and whispered in my ear, "Slightly cracked, crossed in love; speaks very peculiarly; capital chap though." Then crossing to where the Fish was standing, he said, "And this is A. Fish, Esq., the celebrated lecturer on the 'Whichness of the What as compared with the Thatness of the Thus.' He desired to accompany us here in order to

"HIS MAJESTY THE WALLYPUG"

find material for a new lecture which he is preparing upon the 'Perhapness of the Improbable.' He's awfully clever," he whispered impressively.

"I'm sure I'm delighted to see you all," I said, shaking hands with each one till I came to the Fish, who held out a fin. " Er-er-how do you do?" I stammered, somewhat taken aback by this strange proceeding.

"Quide well with the egscebtiod of a slide cold id by head," said the Fish. "I'b subjecd to theb, you doe. It's beig id the water so butch, I fadcy," and he *smiled*.

I don't know if you have ever seen a fish smile, but if not I may tell you that it is a very curious sight.

"I suppose you can manage to put us up here for a month or two?" calmly suggested the Doctor-in-Law after a pause.

"Dear me," I exclaimed in alarm, "I don't think my housekeeper could possibly—"

"Why not ask her?" suggested the Doctor-in-Law, touching the bell.

A moment or two afterwards a knock at the door announced that Mrs. Putchy was there.

"Oh, Mrs. Putchy," I said, stepping just

outside, "these gentlemen, er—that is to say, his Majesty the Wallypug of Why and suite, have honoured me with a visit, and I am anxious if possible to offer them such hospitality as my poor home affords. Do you think that we could manage anyhow to find room for them, for a few days at any rate?"

Now Mrs. Putchy is a very remarkable woman, and I have never known her to show the slightest surprise at anything, and, so far from seeming alarmed at the prospect of having to entertain such notable visitors, she seemed positively delighted.

"His Majesty of Why, sir? How charming! Of course we must do our best, and how fortunate that I put on my best gown to-day, isn't it? Dear me, and shall I be presented to his Majesty?"

"Certainly, Mrs. Putchy, if you wish it," I said. "In fact, if you will call General Mary Jane, I will introduce you both, as you represent my entire household."

Mrs. Putchy disappeared, returning almost immediately, followed by the servant, General Mary Jane, with her mouth wide open, and accompanied by the cat, who rejoices in the extraordinary name of Mrs. Mehetable Murchison. These members of my household were duly presented to the Wallypug. Mrs. Putchy made her curtsey with great dignity, but General Mary Jane was so overcome at the thought of being presented to royalty that she fell flat on her hands and knees in her humility, while Mrs. Mehetable Murchison, realizing, no doubt, the truth of the old saying that "a cat may look at a king," went up and sharpened her claws on the Wallypug's legs in the most friendly manner possible.

It was when the cat caught sight of A. Fish, Esq., that she completely lost her presence of mind, and with arched back and bristling fur glared at him in amazement.

"Priddy pussy, cub alog thed," said the Fish, stooping down and trying to stroke her with one of his fins; but Mrs. Mehetable Murchison, with a startled glance, tore out of the room, showing every sign of alarm.

"And she's so fond of fish too, as a rule, ain't she, mum?" remarked General Mary Jane, who had somewhat overcome the awe with which she had at first regarded the presence of royalty.

"Fod of fish?" repeated A. Fish, Esq., inquiringly. "What do you mead?"

"Why, you see, sir," explained Mrs. Putchy, "we often have fish for dinner—er—that is to say—er—a-hem!"

"PRIDDY PUSSY"

The Fish was glaring at her in a horrified way, and Mrs. Putchy had become quite nervous.

"Let's change the subject," suggested the Doctor-in-Law, to our great relief. "The most important question for the moment is, where are we all going to sleep?"

This gave Mrs. Putchy an opportunity for exercising her wonderful ability for management, and after arranging for the Wallypug to have the spare bedroom, and the Doctor-in-Law to have my room, I was to have a bed made up in the study, while the Jubilee Rhymester was to sleep in the attic, One-and-Nine was to have a box under the stairs, and there only remained A. Fish, Esq., to dispose of.

"There is the bathroom, mum," suggested General Mary Jane brilliantly; "we could put a lid on the bath and make up a bed there."

"Bedder sdill, fill id with wadter, ad thed I could sleeb *in* id," suggested the Fish.

"Oh yes, of course!" said Mrs. Putchy, "and now I must go and see about the supper." And, with a low curtsey to the Wallypug, the admirable little woman hurried out, followed by General Mary Jane, who gave a nervous little bob when she reached the door.

They had scarcely disappeared before One-and-Nine came up to me and whispered:

"I am muchly impressionated by that lady with the most militaryish name who has just gone out. Can you kindly inform me is she detached?"

"Detached?" I inquired in bewilderment. "What ever do you mean?"

"If a person is not attached to anyone else, they are detached, I suppose, are they not?" said One-and-Nine rather impatiently.

"Well, if you put it that way, I suppose they are," I replied, laughing. "You mean, has she a sweetheart? Well, really I don't know. I have an idea though that Mrs. Putchy does not allow followers."

"Then I shall considerize my prospectuousness with great hopefulosity!" remarked the soldier with considerable dignity, walking back to the Wallypug's chair.

"What does he say?" asked the Jubilee Rhymester. "He is a little bit cracked, you know. Could you make out what he was driving at?"

"Oh, yes, I could understand within a little what he meant," I replied. "He seems to have fallen in love with General Mary Jane at first sight, from what I can gather."

"Really! Dear me! He is always doing that sort of thing, do you know, and he generally asks me to write poems for him when he gets into that state. I have written

HIS MAJESTY AND SUITE ARRIVE

as many as 137 odes in one month on his behalf."

"Good gracious," I replied, "and does he pay you well for them?"

"Pay me!" exclaimed the Jubilee Rhymester, staring at me in surprise. "Of course not. Do people ever get paid for writing poetry?"

"Why, yes, to be sure they do," I answered.

"Well, I've never heard of such a thing in all my life," said the Jubilee Rhymester; "I always thought that poets had to pay to have their verses used at all, and that that was why they were always so poor while they were alive. Of course I knew that people sometimes made a fuss about them after they were dead, but I have never heard of such a thing as a live poet being paid for his work."

"Nonsense," I replied; "I believe that quite a lot of money is sometimes paid by the magazines and other papers for poems and verses."

"Well, I am delighted to hear it," said the Jubilee Rhymester, "and I shall certainly start writing to-morrow. I have no doubt whatever that I shall make my fortune before I go back to Zum."

Shortly after this Mrs. Putchy announced that supper was served, and a little later my guests retired to rest, being thoroughly tired out with their long journey. I sat up in my study a little while longer to smoke a pipe, but was just thinking of going to bed when there was a tap at the door and the Doctor-in-Law entered.

"I say, I thought I had better come and arrange with you about money matters," he said; "I didn't like to mention such things before the others. Now then," he continued, "how much are you going to pay us for staying with you?"

"Pay *you*!" I gasped. "What on earth do you mean?"

"Well, you see, it will be a great thing for you to have such distinguished visitors, don't you know, and you ought to be quite willing to pay liberally for the honour," said the Doctor-in-Law, smiling amiably.

Now Girlie had told me what a greedy, avaricious person the Doctor-in-Law really was, despite his benevolent appearance, but this cool cheek almost took my breath away. I was determined, however, to let him see at

HIS MAJESTY AND SUITE ARRIVE 17

once that I was not to be imposed upon, so I said as firmly as I could, "Now, look here, Mr. Doctor-in-Law, please understand once and for all, that as you were all so kind to my little friend Girlie when she was at Why, I am quite willing to entertain his Majesty the Wallypug, and the rest of you, to the very best of my ability, but as for paying you for being here, the idea is absurd—impossible!"

"ID QUIDE GAVE BE A TURN"

Just then a terrific hullabaloo in the passage caused us both to run to the door. We could hear that the noise proceeded from the bathroom, and, hurrying to the door, we found

A. Fish, Esq., sitting up in the water shouting for help, while Mrs. Mehetable Murchison and a whole group of her feline friends were out on the tiles, glaring through the window.

"Dear be, dear be," panted the Fish, when he saw us, "I'b so frighteded, just look at all those cats. I had beed to sleeb ad was just dreabig that sobeone was sayig, "Mrs. Behetable Burchison is *so* fod of fish, and we ofted have fish for didder," whed I woke ub and saw all those horrible cats lookig id ad the widdow; id quide gave be a turn. Do drive theb away please."

We soon did this, and, pulling down the blinds, we left A. Fish, Esq., to his dreams and soon afterwards retired to rest ourselves.

CHAPTER II

THE NEXT DAY'S ADVENTURES

WHEN I entered the breakfast room the next morning I found that the Wallypug and the Doctor-in-Law had been up for some time, and were both gazing out of the window with the greatest of interest.

"I hope your Majesty slept well," I remarked to the Wallypug as I approached them.

"Very well indeed, thank you," he replied smilingly. "The Doctor-in-Law and myself have just been saying that we are sure to have an enjoyable visit here. We have been greatly interested in the man-machines going past. We have never seen anything like them before."

"The man-machines!" I exclaimed, puzzled to know whatever he could mean.

"Yes, the men with wheels instead of legs, you know."

"Oh, you mean the bicyclists, I replied, laughing. "Have you really never seen any before?"

"No, indeed," replied his Majesty. "Are they born with wheels on, or do they grow afterwards?"

I laughed, and fortunately just then the youngster opposite, who always rides to school on his bicycle, came out of doors wheeling his machine, and I was able to explain to the Wallypug the principle upon which they worked.

"Dear me; the Doctor-in-Law told me that the machinery was part of the man, but now I see that it is separate. And he charged me sixpence for the information too," he complained, looking reproachfully at the Doctor-in-Law.

"Charged you sixpence!" I cried.

"Yes," replied the poor Wallypug. "He offered to tell me all about them for sixpence, and as I was really very curious to know I gave it to him, and then he informed me that they were a peculiar race of people who came from Coventry, and who were all born with wheels instead of legs."

THE NEXT DAY'S ADVENTURES

"Take your old sixpence then, if you are going to make all that fuss about it," said the Doctor-in-Law, crossly, throwing the coin down on the table and walking out of the room in a huff. "I'm sure I did read somewhere that they came from Coventry," he added, popping his head in at the door and then slamming it violently after him.

The boy opposite was still riding up and down the road, and I made up my mind that although I had never spoken to him before, I would ask him to let the Wallypug examine his bicycle more closely.

"With pleasure," he replied, raising his hat politely to the Wallypug, when I had explained who he was; "and if his Majesty would like to try it he is quite welcome to do so."

The Doctor-in-Law's curiosity had so far overcome his ill-humour that, when he saw us talking to the boy, he came forward and offered to help the Wallypug to mount.

"I really don't think he had better," I said, "he might damage the machine."

"Oh no, he won't hurt it, I'm sure," said the boy generously; and so with our united assistance the Wallypug got on to the bicycle, and after a few preliminary wobblings started off in fine style. Faster and faster he went, clinging desperately to the handle-bars, till we, who were running beside him, could no longer keep pace with him.

THE START

"I can't stop," we heard him shout; and a moment later he charged straight at a large stone and half a brick which lay in the middle of the roadway.

Poor Wallypug! The sudden impact threw him right over the handle-bars, and he landed in a huddled heap on his hands and knees in the gutter. The machine flew in half, and the

THE NEXT DAY'S ADVENTURES 23

front portion careered madly away by itself till stopped by the kerb.

We hurried up to his Majesty to discover if he was much hurt, but, with the exception of a few scratches on his hands and knees and a thorough shaking, he seemed to have come off pretty well.

THE FINISH

"I suppose we can't stick it together again?" he inquired, gazing ruefully at the broken bicycle, and I was obliged to tell him that there was not much chance of our doing so. The boy to whom it belonged bravely made the best of the matter, especially when I told him that the next half-holiday he had I would take him to Holborn to choose another one in its place.

And when I discovered that he had a half-holiday that very afternoon, it was arranged that General Mary Jane should order a carriage at the livery stable, and that we should all drive to the city after luncheon.

The Wallypug, after a good wash and a hearty breakfast, went to his room to lie down for an hour or two to recover from the effects of his accident, and I was just answering my morning letters when there was a knock at the study door, and the Rhymester entered.

"I sat up most of the night writing poetry," he remarked, "and I have just brought you one or two specimens. The first one is called 'The Ode of a Toad.' Perhaps I had better read it to you. My writing is rather peculiar," and he began as follows:

HIPPETY-HOPPETY-PLOP

THE ODE OF A TOAD.

There was once an old toad who lived under a tree,
    Hippety hop—Flippety flop,
And his head was as bald as bald could be,

THE NEXT DAY'S ADVENTURES

He was deaf as a post and could hardly see,
But a giddy and frivolous toad was he,
    With his hippety-hoppety-plop.

And he gambolled and danced on the village green,
    Hippety hop—Flippety flop,
In a way that had never before been seen,
Tho' he wasn't so young as once he had been,
And the people all wondered whate'er he could mean,
    With his hippety-hoppety-plop.

But the old chap kept bobbing about just the same,
    Hippety hop—Flippety flop,
Till everyone thought he *must* make himself lame,
And not a soul ever could find out his aim,
In keeping up such a ridiculous game,
    As his hippety-hoppety-plop.

Some said he was mad, tho' as mild as a dove,
    Hippety hop—Flippety flop,
And as the result of a push or a shove,
Was a little bit cracked in the storey above,
But I fancy myself the old boy was in love,
    With his hippety-hoppety-plop.

"There! What do you think of it?" he asked when he had finished.

"Well, candidly, I'm afraid not very much," I replied; "and what on earth do you call it an ode for?"

"Why, you see, ode went so well with the word toad. I was going to call it 'Ode to a

Toad,' but it isn't *to* a toad at all, though it's about a toad. Ah! by the bye, I might call it 'A Toad's Ode,' mightn't I? I think that sounds very jolly." He altered the title in pencil.

"I have another which I think you will say is very touching." And after getting his handkerchief out in case he should be moved to tears, he began:

"I LOVE BUT THEE"

THE BALLADE OF A BUN.

Don't talk to me of "Sally Lunn,"
   Or toasted tea-cake nice and hot,
I do not care for either one
   A single solitary jot;
My heart is fixed and changeth not,
   In all the world—whate'er I see,
And rich or poor—whate'er my lot—
   Oh! penny bun, I love but thee.

For thy dear sake all cakes I shun
   Smeared o'er with jam. No apricot
Or greengage tart my heart hath won;
   Their sweetness doth but cloy and clot.
What marmalade in fancy pot
   Or cream meringue, though fair it be,
Thine image e'er can mar or blot?
   Oh! penny bun, I love but thee.

I vowed to cherish thee, or none
  (Such love thy simple charms begot),
When first I saw thee, precious one ;
  And now to some sweet lonely spot,
Some shady dell or mossy grot,
  Come let us hasten, you and me,
And I will eat you like a shot ;
  Oh ! penny bun, I love but thee.

Envoy.

Small boys or girls that homeward trot
  From school in time for early tea,
This moral ne'er must be forgot :
  "Love penny buns, and they'll love thee."

"Isn't it affecting?" he inquired, wiping his eyes when he had finished.

"Well, perhaps I didn't quite appreciate the pathos of it as I might have done," I answered, trying hard not to laugh. "You see I was paying so much attention to the scansion. I find that you have altered the refrain in the Envoy. Surely that's not correct, is it?"

"Oh, you are a great deal too particular," remarked the Rhymester crossly. "Why, I should think from the Doctor-in-Law's description of a critic that you must be one."

"What did he say a critic was?" I asked.

"Why, he said a critic was a person who found fault with another, for not doing what he was unable to do himself. And he charged me fourpence three-farthings for the information, and as I only had fourpence halfpenny I have to pay him the odd farthing when I sell some of my poems. Can you tell me how I can set to work about it?"

"Well, I hardly know," I replied, "unless you send them to the editors of the various magazines. They may take them, but you must not be disappointed if some of them are rejected. You see they cannot possibly print everything that is sent to them."

There were several magazines in the study, and I suggested that the Rhymester should make a list of the addresses of the various editors, and he was busy about that till luncheon time.

At half-past two the carriage came to the door, and goodness only knows what General Mary Jane must have told the livery stable people about the Wallypug, for, evidently anxious to send an equipage worthy of royalty, they had painted an enormous monogram in gold on the sides of the carriage, while the

THE NEXT DAY'S ADVENTURES

coachman was resplendent in blue plush and gold lace, with silk stockings and a powdered wig.

The Wallypug was delighted when he saw this elaborate turn-out, and so were the others,

"EQUIPAGEOUS GRANDIOSITY"

for I overheard One-and-Nine murmuring something about "equipageous grandiosity," as he climbed up to the seat beside the coachman. When the Wallypug, the Doctor-in-Law, A. Fish, Esq., and the Rhymester, were seated, there was no room left for the boy and myself, so we followed behind in a modest dog-cart, which was hurriedly procured from the livery stable. Many were the wondering glances bestowed upon the carriage, with its somewhat remarkable burden, as we drove along through Kensington to the Gardens. And everywhere our appearance was hailed with enthusiasm, people being evidently under the impression that the Wallypug was one of the royal guests invited to the Jubilee festivities. Who could he be? That was decidedly the question which everyone was asking, and I could not quite determine who was causing the greater sensation, the Wallypug or A. Fish, Esq. These two individuals, however, comported themselves with the calmest dignity, only the Doctor-in-Law seemed flurried by the attention which they attracted, and smiled and bowed right and left, whether the people took any notice of him or not.

As we approached Hyde-Park corner attention was diverted from the Wallypug's carriage by the fact that *another* royal equipage had entered the Park gates; and as the Princess passed us, an amused glance and a whispered conversation with the other occupant of the carriage showed that the Wallypug's extraordinary party had not escaped Her Royal Highness's attention.

After going once round the Park we went

out at the Marble Arch and along Oxford Street to Holborn, our progress through the crowded streets everywhere attracting the most excited interest. And when we stopped before one of the large bicycle *depôts* in Holborn the crowd around the carriage was so large that the policeman had quite a difficulty in preventing a block in the traffic. Our business was soon transacted, and, having secured an excellent machine for the boy in place of the one which his Majesty had damaged in the morning, we drove back to Kensington without further adventure.

The Wallypug's curiosity, however, was so awakened by what he had seen that, as soon as we had been refreshed by a cup of afternoon tea, he suggested that we should go out for a walk; accordingly the whole party proceeded to Kensington Gardens, followed by a curious and somewhat derisive crowd of small boys, who would insist upon advising the Wallypug to "get his hair cut." Now, I happened to know, from what Girlie had told me about her adventures in Why, that the Wallypug, though a kind of king, had to do as his people directed and not as he liked, and that when he had presented a petition in Parliament to be allowed to have his hair cut, they had divided upon the subject, and so he had only been allowed to have *half* of it cut, and as the long half had by this time grown very long indeed, he certainly did look rather remarkable; that was no excuse though for the street boys' rudeness, and his Majesty very wisely took no notice of them. A. Fish, Esq., came in for the greatest amount of attention, and when a few drops of rain began to fall, and he put up an umbrella for fear that he should get wet, the crowd became so excited that the Doctor-in-Law wisely suggested that a return should be made. His Majesty, however, was bent upon sight-seeing, and so the party separated, the Doctor-in-Law, A. Fish, Esq., and One-and-Nine going home, while the rest of us continued our walk. When we reached the Gardens, the Wallypug was greatly interested in seeing the palace where the Queen was born, and said that he should certainly petition his Parliament to allow him to have soldiers walk up and down before the gates of his palace, like those which he saw here. He admired greatly Princess Louise's

FOR FEAR HE SHOULD GET WET

C

statue of the Queen, which stands in front of the palace, and said he couldn't imagine wherever they could have got all the white sugar from to make it with, and I think that he was inclined to disbelieve me when I told him that it was not made of sugar at all, but of white marble; for he said that if that were the case he couldn't think why they wanted to put such high railings around it, as no one would wish to carry away a marble statue of that size, whereas, if it were sugar, as he suggested, why, of course, the railings were there to prevent the children from climbing up and breaking off little pieces to eat.

The Round Pond and the little model ships interested His Majesty most of all though, I fancy, and he spent quite a long time admiring them, until, while assisting a small boy to get his ship ashore, he had the misfortune to slip into the water himself, and had to be fished out with the assistance of a boathook.

His Majesty certainly did not look either dignified or regal as he stood on the bank saturated with water, and his royal robes clinging about him in the most woe-begone manner —and as the crowd had greatly increased, I was very glad to get the poor Wallypug into a cab and drive home.

On our way there, the Rhymester, being very much afraid of getting his clothes wet, sat in the furthest corner of the cab and

HIS MAJESTY HAS AN ACCIDENT

amused himself by writing a verse on the subject of his Majesty's misfortune, which read somehow like this:

> "King George I've heard is King of Greece,
>   But since this luckless slipping,
> The Wallypug I do declare
>   Should be the King of *Dripping*."

I think his Majesty thought it rather unkind of the Rhymester to make fun of him in this way, but before he had time to think much about the matter, we had arrived at our destination, and to my great surprise I could see a vast crowd collected at the doors of the building in which my flat is situated.

CHAPTER III

SUNDRY SMALL HAPPENINGS

WHATEVER could it all mean? The Doctor-in-Law stood on the steps, calling out, "Walk up, walk up, ladies and gentlemen, and see the Talking Fish," while large posters were pasted on the walls, bearing the words, "Admission Sixpence" and "One day only."

The Commissionaire who usually stands at the door was looking very surprised and angry, while the page boy was grinning all over his face. Whatever was happening? I hastily paid the cabman, and followed by the Wally-pug made my way through the crowd to the entrance.

"Admission sixpence each," said the Doctor-in-Law, holding out his hand.

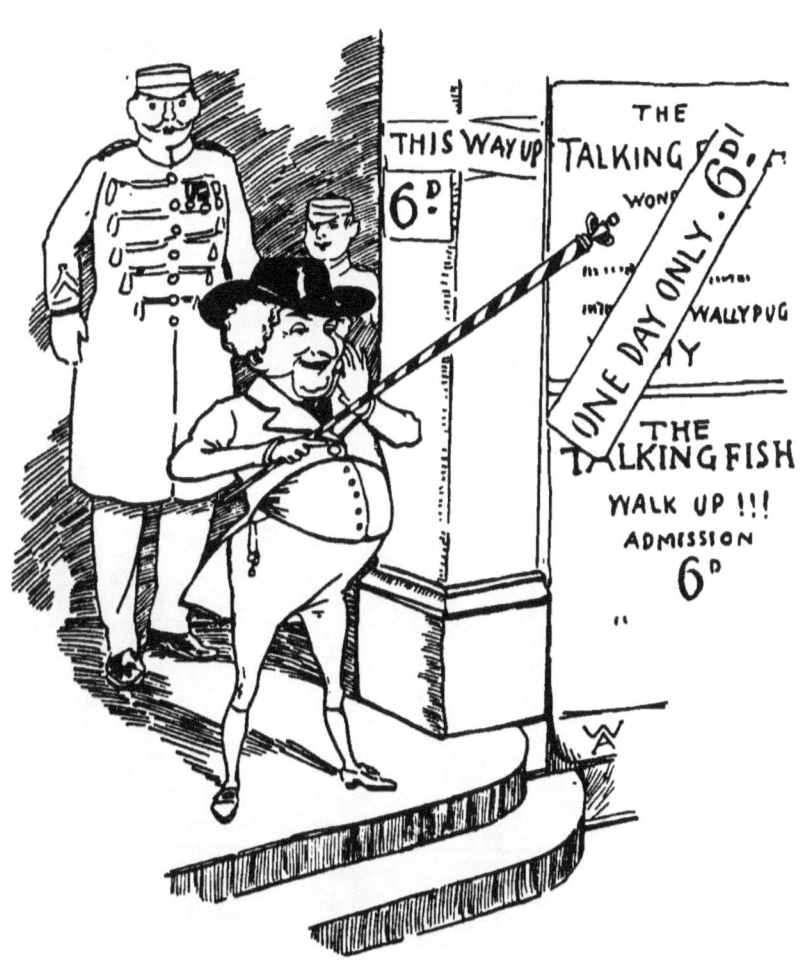

"WALK UP, WALK UP, LADIES AND GENTLEMEN"

SUNDRY SMALL HAPPENINGS 41

"What do you mean?" I replied, "and what is all this crowd doing here?"

"Admission sixpence each!" repeated the Doctor-in-Law stubbornly, not taking the least notice of my questions, and holding his wand across the doorway so that I could not get in.

"Nonsense!" I cried; "I'm not going to pay to go into my own house."

"Pay for the Wallypug then and I'll let you in free," said the little man insinuatingly.

"I shall do nothing of the sort," I cried, pushing past him and hurrying up the stairs.

To my surprise I found my rooms occupied by strangers. Sergeant One-and-Nine was reciting some of the Rhymester's poems in the dining room to three deaf old ladies, two of whom had ear trumpets, while A. Fish, Esq., was holding a kind of *levée* in my study, seated in a chair placed on the writing table, and was surrounded by an admiring crowd of people who were asking all sorts of questions.

Mrs. Putchy met me at the door.

"Oh, sir!" she exclaimed. "I'm so glad you've come home. I haven't known what to do with all these people."

"But what does it all mean, Putchy?" I

inquired. "What are they doing here at all?"

"Why, you see, sir!" said Mrs. Putchy, "Mr. Doctor-in-Law found that A. Fish, Esq., was attracting a good deal of attention out of doors, and he thought that it would be a capital idea to have a kind of show here and charge sixpence admission to see him; and if there's been one, I'm sure there's been a hundred people up here this afternoon. The remarks they've been making too, and the questions they've been asking. Why, one old lady, sir, wanted to know how much you paid A. Fish, Esq., a week, and if I was *quite* sure that you gave him enough to eat. They've broken three chairs too, and that little Venetian glass vase that stood on the bracket in the corner. And just now I caught some little boys tearing pictures out of one of those illustrated books you brought home last week."

Here was a pretty state of affairs. The strangers had by this time left A. Fish, Esq., and had collected around the poor Wallypug, who had been waiting in his wet clothing in the hall, and I was obliged to politely but firmly insist upon them at once leaving the

SUNDRY SMALL HAPPENINGS

house, telling them that their money would be returned at the door.

"I should think so, indeed," said one angry-looking stout lady. "Why, the whole thing is a fraud and you ought to be thoroughly ashamed of yourself. Talking fish indeed! I don't believe he's a fish at all—at any rate, not what I call a 'fish,'" and she flounced down the stairs only to return a moment or two afterwards to say, "I thought you said that we were to have our money back."

"So you are, madam," I replied.

"Well, why don't you see that we get it then? That man downstairs refuses to give me any money. The whole thing is a swindle. But I don't mean to be defrauded in this way, I can tell you."

I went downstairs and told the Doctor-in-Law that he must at once return everyone their money, and this after a great deal of grumbling he did, while the Commissionaire and the page boy tore down the posters outside the door at my request.

I explained to the Doctor-in-Law that this sort of thing must not occur again, and made him promise that he would never again use my rooms as a place in which to hold a show.

I really felt rather annoyed about it, for I could not imagine whatever the neighbours would think of me for permitting such a scene to take place in my rooms, but it evidently was useless now to say anything more about it.

The next morning, despite the wetting which the Wallypug had received at the Round Pond, his thoughts still ran upon boating, and nothing would satisfy his Majesty but that he should go for a row. I suggested Richmond as the best place to start from, and so we drove over Hammersmith Bridge and across Barnes Common.

Arrived at Richmond we had no difficulty in securing a nice boat.

"I'll row for one," said his Majesty.

"And I for another," said the Rhymester.

"Very well then," I replied. "Perhaps the Doctor-in-Law will steer, and so we will manage very nicely."

Quite a large crowd had collected to see us start, and perhaps that is what made the Wallypug so nervous; as it was, as soon as

HIS MAJESTY FELL BACKWARDS

we pushed off, his Majesty fell backwards with his feet sticking up above the seat, while the Rhymester stuck one oar deep down into the water and pulled it with all his might, while the other flourished about in the air.

The Doctor-in-Law's idea of steering consisted in pulling first one string and then the other, and so we did not get along very well just at first.

When the Wallypug had picked himself up from the bottom of the boat, however, and the Rhymester and he made another attempt, I think we should have got along fairly well if the Doctor-in-Law, in trying to get out of the way of a passing boat, had not steered us into the bank, where we stuck fast in the mud till someone on the footpath very kindly pushed us off again. After that I thought it best to take the oars myself, and his Majesty steered under my direction. In this way we managed to get a little way past Teddington Lock by luncheon time, and having found an *eyot* with no one on it we went ashore and unpacked the hamper of good things which we had brought with us.

It was a beautiful day, and I think that we all enjoyed the picnic immensely. I know that I did for one, and so, I think, did his Majesty, for after the meal he laid aside his crown and royal robes and made himself comfortable on the grass under the trees, and looked thoroughly happy with a big cigar in his mouth.

HIS MAJESTY ENJOYS HIMSELF

A. Fish, Esq., busied himself in preparing notes for his lecture on the "Perhapness of the Improbable," and the Doctor-in-Law, having piled all the cushions in the boat at one end, threw himself upon them and read the newspaper.

In this way the afternoon passed very comfortably, and the Rhymester, after scribbling upon several pieces of paper, came and read to me a poem which had been inspired by our beautiful surroundings; he called it

SOUL YEARNINGS.

The water's as wet as wet can be,
  And the trees, and the grass, are green,
While the little birds sing and the fishes swim;
  'Tis a most delightful scene.

It makes me yearn for I don't know what,
  To come from I don't know where,
And take me away to the thingummybob
  And the what-you-may-call-'ems there;

and he told me that beautiful scenery always affected him in that way.

It was now time for us to be thinking about getting back, especially as I should have to do all of the rowing. So we got into the boat again, and I rowed back as far as Twickenham, where we stopped at Eel-pie Island to have some tea. While we were waiting for it to

AN UNFORTUNATE VOLLEY

be prepared, we began a game of tennis, but were obliged to leave off, as an unfortunate volley of the Doctor-in-Law's caught the Wallypug on the nose, and so his Majesty declined to play any more.

We persuaded him to join us at cricket, though, having found some stumps and a bat and ball in an outhouse on the Island, and

"OUT"

got on very well for some time till, at a shout of "out, leg before wicket," the Wallypug (who had caught the ball very nicely on his shin) fell forward on to the Doctor-in-Law, crushing his hat well over his eyes, and ruffling his temper considerably.

In fact, I was very glad that tea was announced just then, for I feared that there was going to be a bother, and, as it was, the Doctor-in-Law kept scowling at his Majesty very fiercely.

"I shall make him pay for it," declared the little man, and, during tea, which we had at wicker tables by the river's edge, he was busy making out an account, which later he handed with great solemnity to the Wallypug. His Majesty apparently could not understand it, and passed it on to me. On examination, I found it to be worded as follows:

His Majesty the Wallypug of Why,
  In account with
    The Doctor-in-Law.

			£	s.	d.
To damage of one hat,	-	-	0	7	6
„ Physical injury,	-	-	0	2	0
„ Moral deterioration,	-	-	15	6	9
			£22	17	8
„ 3 per cent. discount for cash,	-		3	6	2
			£26	4	11

"What do you mean by moral deterioration?" demanded the Wallypug.

"Oh, I don't know. Same as other people do, I suppose," said the Doctor-in-Law. "It's always charged now, I believe. I read something about it in the papers this afternoon,"

"But the addition is all wrong," I expostulated.

"No, it isn't," replied the Doctor-in-Law, rudely snatching the document from me and putting it into his pocket-book, "and if it is, it's nothing to do with you. I shall charge it in our expenses, which the people of Why have undertaken to pay, so there." And the avaricious little fellow ran off to the boat, which we afterwards found he had been letting out on hire to small boys at a penny a head.

The return journey was accomplished without any remarkable incidents, and on reaching home I found a very pressing invitation from Girlie's mother for the whole party to attend her "At Home" the next day.

It appears that this lady had called upon me while we were out, and Mrs. Putchy had told her of the Wallypug's arrival.

His Majesty was good enough to say that he should be delighted to accept, and so I wrote off at once to say that she might expect us.

CHAPTER IV

LOST

WE had a terrible fright the next morning, for the poor dear Wallypug got lost, and for some time we could not imagine what had become of him.

It happened in this way: directly after breakfast his Majesty said that he should like to go for a walk and look at the shops.

"I'm not going," declared the Doctor-in-Law. "I have some *very* important letters to write."

We all looked up in surprise, for we did not know that the Doctor-in-Law had any other acquaintances in London.

"Letters from which I hope to derive a princely income," continued the little man grandly; "and, therefore, I have no time for such foolishness as looking into shop windows."

"He's afraid thad he bight have to sped sub buddy," remarked A. Fish, Esq.

"Nothing of the sort," replied the Doctor-in-Law, turning very red though.

"Well, don't waste time talking about it; let's go if we are going," said the Rhymester; and so, as I also had some correspondence to attend to, it was arranged that the Wallypug, the Rhymester, and A. Fish, Esq., should go for a little stroll by themselves. I had some doubts in my own mind as to the advisability of letting them go alone, but they promised not to go beyond Kensington Gardens, and to wait for me there just inside the gates.

After they had gone I settled down to my letter-writing, and was getting along nicely when the Doctor-in-Law interrupted me with:

"I say, I wish you would let me have about twenty sheets of note-paper, will you, please?"

"Twenty!" I exclaimed in surprise.

"Yes, twenty," said the Doctor-in-Law. "Or you had better make it a quire while you are about it."

I thought the quickest way to get rid of him was to give him the paper, so I got up and got it for him.

"And a packet of envelopes, please," he said, as I handed it to him.

"Anything else?" I asked rather sarcastically.

"Stamps!" he replied, calmly holding out his hand.

"Well, really—" I expostulated.

"Oh, halfpenny ones will do. You're surely not so mean as to mind tenpence, are you?"

"I don't think I'm mean, but—"

"Hand them over then, and don't waste so much time talking," said the little man impatiently, and so, just to get rid of him, I gave him the stamps and sat down to my letters again.

I had hardly begun when he came back.

"Don't you take any other newspapers than these?" he demanded, showing me a handful.

"No, I don't, and I think it's rather extravagant of me to have those," I replied.

"Well, then, how do you suppose that I am going to manage? I want at least five other papers, and it's *most* important that I should have them."

"You might buy them," I suggested.

"They are so dear," he grumbled.

"Well, why don't you go to the Public Library then?" I suggested. "You know where it is, and you could see all of the papers there, you know."

"Ah, a capital idea," he said, putting on his hat and going out.

"Now," I thought, "I shall have peace at last."

I was not left undisturbed long though, for a few minutes later Mrs. Putchy came to the door.

"Oh, please, sir, will you go down? Mr. Doctor-in-Law is having such a bother with the postman."

I hurried out, and found the little man very angry indeed.

"This postman won't give me a letter," he cried when he saw me.

"Perhaps he hasn't one for you," I answered.

"But I saw him giving them away all down the street for nothing," persisted the Doctor-in-Law. "And when I asked him in a civil way for one, he refused to give it to me. It's no use for him to say he hasn't one, when he has a whole packet in his hand now, and a lot more in his bag, no doubt. Are you going to give me a letter or not?" he continued, turning to the postman.

"ARE YOU GOING TO GIVE ME A LETTER OR NOT?"

"No, sir," continued the man, smiling. "I haven't any for you."

"Very well, then," said the Doctor-in-Law decidedly, "I shall certainly write to the Queen and tell her that if she employs you any longer I shall take all my custom away, and I shall not send the twenty letters, that I intended writing to-day, off at all."

I endeavoured to explain to the little man that the postman could not possibly give him a letter if he had not one addressed to him.

"Oh, that's all nonsense," he exclaimed, going off in a huff. "Of course you would take his part."

Before I could settle down to work again the Rhymester and A. Fish, Esq., returned.

"Where's the Wallypug?" I demanded.

"Oh, he's coming by the next 'bus," said the Rhymester. "Haven't you had any rain here?"

"No," I replied.

"Oh, we had quidt a sharb shower," said A. Fish, Esq., "ad I was afraid of gettig wet, so we stopped a 'bus—there was odly roob for two though, ad the Wallypug said thad he would cub od by the dext."

"I hope he will get home all right," I said anxiously. "I don't think you ought to have left his Majesty by himself.

"Oh! it's only a little way," said the Rhymester; "he's sure to get home all right."

An hour passed and there was no signs of

"SO WE STOPPED A 'BUS"

the Wallypug. I now began to get seriously anxious.

It would, of course, be the easiest thing in the world for his Majesty to take the wrong 'bus, and be taken goodness knows where.

I couldn't think what was best to be done. The Rhymester suggested sending the Crier out, but I never remembered having seen one at Kensington, and at last, after searching for some time ourselves in Kensington Gardens, and making inquiries in High Street, and failing to glean any tidings of his Majesty, I thought it best to go to the Police Station.

Here I found a very important-looking official in uniform, with a big book in front of him.

"What is it?" he inquired, glaring at me fiercely.

"I've called to know if you could assist me in finding a friend who, I fear, has lost his way," I replied.

The official did not answer me, but reached down another large book.

"What's his name?" he inquired gruffly.

"His name? Oh—er—his name is—er—that is to say he is the—" I had not the least idea what the Wallypug's name really was, so I couldn't very well say.

"What's his name?" shouted the official. "I'll ask you what he *is* presently."

"Well, I'm very sorry, but I really do not know his name."

The man glanced at me very suspiciously.

"You said he was a friend of yours—it's a very odd thing that you don't know his name. What is he?"

"He's a—a—Wallypug," I stammered. "That is to say he—er—"

"Wallypug!" exclaimed the man contemptuously. "What's that?"

"Why, it's a kind of king, you know," I explained, feeling that the explanation was rather a lame one.

"A *kind* of king!" exclaimed the police officer. "Explain yourself."

"Well, I'm afraid I can't explain more clearly than that," I replied. "This gentleman has been staying with me for a couple of days, and went out this morning and lost his way."

"Where did he come from?" asked the man.

"Why," I answered.

"Why? Because I want to know," he shouted. "Don't let me have any further prevarication. Where did the man, or Wallypug, or whatever you call him, come from?"

"From Why. From a place called Why, you know," I repeated.

"I *don't* know," said the officer. "I've never heard of such a place. Where is it?"

"Well, really," I said, "I'm very sorry, but I cannot tell you. I don't know myself."

"This is *very* remarkable," said the man, glaring at me through his glasses. "You don't know your friend's name; you call him a Wallypug, and can't explain what that is, you don't know where he comes from—perhaps you can tell me how he reached your house?"

I was now really in a fix, for how could I tell this man that his Majesty had stepped out of a picture.

I thought the best thing to do was to hold my tongue.

"How did he come?" repeated the officer. "By train?"

I shook my head.

"By steamer?"

I shook my head again.

"Did he drive?—or come on a bicycle, or walk?"

I remained silent.

The police officer stared at me for a moment or two, waiting for my answer.

"Look here, young man," said he at last, evidently very angry indeed. "It strikes me that you are having a game with me. You had better go away quietly or I shall be obliged to take you in charge as a lunatic."

"But I assure you that—"

"How was your friend dressed?"

"Oh, he wore a somewhat battered gold crown, and carried an orb and sceptre, and was dressed in knee breeches and a velvet cloak with an ermine collar."

The man gave me a keen glance and then rang a bell. A policeman appeared a moment or two afterwards, and the officer whispered something to him, of which I only caught the words, "harmless lunatic."

"Lunatic, sir; yes, sir. Step this way, please," said the policeman, and before I could realize what had happened I was bundled into a small bare room, and the key was turned in the lock and I was a prisoner.

Here was a pretty state of affairs. The stupid people had mistaken me for a lunatic, and I was no doubt to be locked up here till a doctor arrived.

Of course the only thing for me to do was to sit still and wait as patiently as I could. Fortunately the police people thought of telegraphing to the other stations to find out if anything was known of an escaped lunatic; and from Fulham came the reply, "We have found one ourselves, He calls himself a Wallypug, and is dressed like a second-hand king." This caused inquiries to be made, and eventually I was taken in a cab to Fulham, where we found his Majesty in the charge of the police, he having been found wandering about the Fulham Road quite unable to give what they considered a satisfactory account of himself.

It was most unfortunate that his Majesty should have taken the wrong 'bus, for, not having any money with him, he was set down in a totally strange neighbourhood, and had quite forgotten my address. Of course, now that we had been brought face to face, we had no difficulty in convincing the police people that we were what we represented ourselves to be, and were soon, to our great relief, on our way home again.

"I don't think that I should like to be a policeman," remarked the Wallypug, on our way there.

"No?" I answered. "Why not?"

"They have to catch dogs for a living?" remarked his Majesty solemnly. "There were several brought in while I was waiting, and the policeman who had caught them seemed so pleased about it."

I explained to the Wallypug as well as I was able about the muzzling order, and his Majesty was highly indignant, and when I pointed out several dogs with muzzles on he was more indignant still.

"And are they always obliged to wear those horrible wire cages over their heads?" he inquired.

I told his Majesty that in London the order for wearing them had been in force for some considerable time, and we had a long talk over the matter, his Majesty declaring that he

UNABLE TO GIVE AN ACCOUNT OF HIMSELF

should try and invent a new muzzle which should be more comfortable for the poor dogs.

"Oh, here we are at last," he exclaimed, as we turned the corner near my house. "And there are the others on the steps!"

"Here they are! Here they are!" shouted the Rhymester to the others, and everyone rushed forward to assist his Majesty to alight, seemingly very glad to see us back again.

We were quite as delighted to get back, I can tell you, and I was so relieved at having found the Wallypug that I hadn't the heart to refuse the Doctor-in-Law's request that I would give him ten shillings worth of penny stamps to put into the letters which he had been writing while we had been away, although he would not give me the slightest clue as to what they were wanted for.

CHAPTER V

AN 'AT HOME' AND THE ACADEMY

WE were quite ready for luncheon, as you may imagine, after our morning's adventures, and directly afterwards his Majesty set to work on the new dog's muzzle which he had promised to invent. In about half an hour he had constructed one with which he was intensely delighted, and he persuaded A. Fish, Esq., to try it on that we might see the effect.

It certainly was very simple, but as there was nothing whatever to go over the mouth, I felt sure that it could not possibly be very useful. I did not like to tell his Majesty so though, for he seemed so thoroughly proud of his achievement.

It was now time to go to the 'At Home,' so, wishing to do honour to the occasion, our

AN 'AT HOME' AND THE ACADEMY 71

'State Coach,' as we called it, was sent for, and we drove off in fine style.

There were a great many people invited to meet us, and I could see that there was quite a little flutter of excitement when the Wallypug entered.

IT CERTAINLY WAS VERY SIMPLE

His Majesty, however, in his simple, good-natured way soon put everybody at their ease, and laughed and chattered with the utmost affability.

Girlie and Boy had both been allowed to come into the drawing-room, and Girlie quite claimed the Wallypug as her own particular guest, while Boy renewed his acquaintance with the Rhymester, whom he had met before at Zum, and despite their mother's protests they carried these two members of our party off in triumph to show them their play-room and toys and to talk over old times.

While they were away the Doctor-in-Law made himself very agreeable to the ladies, and I watched him bowing and smiling and chatting, first with one group, then with another, with great amusement. I found out afterwards that he had promised several of them portraits of his Majesty and suite for 2s. 6d. each as soon as they should be taken, and in every case had asked for the money in advance; but the great event of the afternoon was when A. Fish, Esq., wrapped up in Mrs. Putchy's pink woollen shawl, borrowed for the occasion, and surrounded by a group of young ladies, consented after much pressing to deliver part of his lecture on the "Perhapness of the Improbable."

"You bust sed for the Rhymebster though to help be to read id, for by cold is still so bad thad I can'd do id by byself," he explained.

So the Rhymester was sent for, and his

AN 'AT HOME' AND THE ACADEMY 73

Majesty also came down to hear the wonderful lecture. It had been turned into verse by the

A. FISH, ESQ., OBLIGES

Rhymester, who, after an affected attempt to clear his throat, read as follows:

THE PERHAPNESS OF THE IMPROBABLE.

If *this* were that, and *these* were those,
  And *hither* nearer thither,
Why, *which* might be whate'er it chose,
  And *there* be any whither.

Somehow 'twould be the simpler way
  To *dearer* be than cheaper,
And that's why *when* (each other day)
  Would *higher* be than *deeper*.

So *worst* would be the *best* of all,
    And *far more less* than either;
While *short* would certainly be *tall*,
    And therefore thus be neither.

"Beautiful! charming!" echoed all the young ladies at once when he had finished, while one

ABSENT-MINDEDLY SPILT HIS TEA

lady sitting near me exclaimed, "How sweetly simple!" For my own part I thought that it was anything but simple, and caught myself trying to follow the line of argument with the most brain-confusing results.

The Wallypug was greatly distressed when he discovered that while listening to the reading, and looking at the charming young lady with whom he had been conversing, he had absent-mindedly spilt the whole of his cup of tea over her dress.

"You see, they didn't give me a plate to put my cake on," I heard him explain apologetically, "and it *was* so awkward, for my cup would keep slipping about on the saucer.

The young lady smiled very sweetly and assured his Majesty that it didn't matter in the least, and shortly afterwards we left, having stayed, as it was, far beyond the regulation time.

When we arrived home we found a letter addressed to the Rhymester in the letter-box, which in a state of great excitement he tore open with trembling fingers.

Upon reading the contents he burst into tears.

"Poor man, poor man!" he sobbed. "I am so sorry to have caused him so much trouble."

"It is a letter from an Editor," he explained through his tears, "and he is in great distress through not being able to publish my poem. He says he greatly regrets his inability to make use of it! Poor man, he evidently feels it very keenly. I must write and tell him not to be too unhappy about it."

I had some letters to write too, one to a photographer in Regent Street, asking for an appointment the next morning, for I was determined that the Doctor-in-Law should send the promised photographs to the young ladies without delay.

The first thing in the morning came a telegram to say that we could be photographed at eleven o'clock, so, after my guests had made themselves as spruce as possible, we started off and reached there in good time.

It was suggested that the Wallypug should be taken by himself, but when he saw the camera pointed directly at him while the operator disappeared beneath the black cloth, he came to the conclusion that it was too dangerous a machine to be faced with impunity, so he suddenly turned his back upon it, and nervously fled from the room.

It was only by promising that the others should be taken with him that we could get him to sit at all, and even then there was a strained and nervous expression upon his face, which suggested that he was in momentary fear that the thing would "go off."

The Rhymester insisted upon being taken with one of his poems in his hand, the Doctor-in-Law wore his usual complacent smile, and altogether the group was quite a success.

As soon as the "operation," as the Wallypug would insist upon calling it, was over, we went downstairs, his Majesty leading the way, while the Doctor-in-Law stayed behind for a moment to make some arrangements with the photographer about commission. We had intended going home by 'bus, but when we got to the door his Majesty was nowhere to be seen. What could have become of him? We looked up and down the street, but could see no signs of him anywhere; and at last, after hunting about for a considerable time, he was discovered calmly sitting inside a furniture removal van, waiting for it to start, under the impression that it was an omnibus.

"I'm sure this is the right one," he explained, "for it has 'Kensington' printed in large letters on it. Come along, there's plenty of room inside; the conductor and the driver will be here presently, I suppose."

I laughingly explained to his Majesty the mistake which he had made, and we walked on as far as Piccadilly Circus, where we found a 'bus to take us to the Academy, which we intended visiting on our way home. We had not gone far though, when I suddenly remembered that the 22nd June was very close at hand, and that I had better make arrangements for seats to view the Jubilee Procession or I should be too late. So it was arrànged that the Doctor-in-Law should take charge of the party while I went on to the agents to see about the seats. They would have no difficulty in getting home by themselves for the 'buses ran from just outside the Academy doors straight to Kensington, so I felt sure that they would be all right.

"How much is the entrance fee to the Academy?" asked the Doctor-in-Law, as I was getting down from the 'bus.

"A shilling each," I replied, and I saw the little man collecting the money from the others as the 'bus disappeared from view.

I was very fortunate at the agents in being

WAITING FOR IT TO START

AN 'AT HOME' AND THE ACADEMY 81

able to secure a capital window in Piccadilly, and some Stores in the neighbourhood undertook to provide a luncheon and to suitably decorate the window for us.

These arrangements being satisfactorily concluded, I hurried home, and was greatly relieved to find my guests there before me.

"How did you enjoy the Academy?" I inquired.

COULD NOT UNDERSTAND THE CATALOGUE

"Not at all!" said his Majesty decidedly,
"Waste of money, I call it," said the Rhymester, sniffing contemptuously.

"I was dever so disappointed id edythig id all by life!" declared A. Fish, Esq.

"Besides, the catalogue was no good at all," complained his Majesty. "We could make neither head nor tail of it."

The Doctor-in-Law was silent, and it was only by very careful inquiry that I found out that, after pocketing their money, he had taken them to an immense hoarding covered with advertisement posters, and had gammoned them into believing that *that* was the Academy, while it was no wonder that the poor Wallypug could not understand the 'catalogue,' for it was nothing more nor less than an old illustrated stores price list.

It was really too bad of the Doctor-in-Law.

CHAPTER VI

THE JUBILEE

THE few days which elapsed before the memorable 22nd of June passed very quickly, and we were all more or less busy making preparations for the festival. His Majesty would insist upon polishing up his regalia himself in order to do honour to the occasion, and spent hours over his crown with a piece of chamois leather and some whitening till, though somewhat battered by the rough usage it had sustained, it shone quite brilliantly. Mrs. Putchy herself suggested making his Majesty some new red silk rosettes for his shoes, which he very graciously consented to accept. The Doctor-in-Law was always so spick and span that we scarcely noticed any change in his appearance, but the Rhymester had made arrangements with

General Mary Jane to wash, starch, and iron his lace collar, and he remained in his room one entire day while it was being done up. A. Fish, Esq., purchased a necktie of most brilliant colouring, and One-and-Nine touched himself up here and there with some red enamel where his tunic had become shabby in places, so that altogether our party looked very smart as we drove at a very early hour to our seats in Piccadilly. To avoid the crowd we went by way of Bayswater Road, and then passed down Park Lane and through Berkeley Square, in order to reach the back entrance to the house in Piccadilly where I had booked seats. Our gorgeous carriage was everywhere hailed with great delight, being of course mistaken for a portion of the Jubilee procession, and many were the conjectures heard on all sides as to who the Wallypug could possibly be.

WITH SOME RED ENAMEL

Our window was in the centre of the building on the first floor, and we had it all to ourselves. A table at the back of the room was tastefully set out with an excellent cold collation, and in front of the window, which was most elaborately decorated with velvet curtains, flags, and trophies, and which was surmounted by a device which was understood to be the Wallypug's coat-of-arms, a gorgeous, gilded, high-backed chair was placed as a throne for his Majesty, and comfortable seats were also provided for the rest of the party.

The crowd outside greeted our appearance with quite a demonstration, as by the enormous placard outside announcing the name of the decorators, and stating that they were by appointment to his Majesty the Wallypug of Why, of course everybody knew who we were. Indeed, one learned-looking person in the crowd was holding forth to an eager audience, and explaining exactly where Why was situated, and pretending that he had been there, and had seen the Wallypug before, ever so many times.

As the time approached for the procession to pass, the Wallypug became very excited and nervous. "Shall I really see the Queen of England?" he kept asking over and over again. "Do you think she will see me? Will she bow to me? What must I say? Must I keep my crown on or take it off?" and innumerable other questions of the same nature.

Presently the excitement and enthusiasm reached their height, as amid a confused shouting of "Here they are," the Guards in advance came in sight. Slowly the mighty procession, with its innumerable squadrons and bands passed, and at last, after the English and Foreign princes and Eastern potentates, the eight cream-coloured Hanoverian horses, drawing the Jubilee landau, made their appearance, and the Queen was seen, smiling and bowing graciously to the cheering populace. The Doctor-in-Law, in his excitement, scrambled on to the window ledge in order to obtain a better view; the Wallypug loyally waved his crown; while the Rhymester, hurriedly unrolling a lengthy ode which he had written especially for the occasion, began reading it in a loud voice, and, though nobody paid the slightest attention to him, did not desist until long after the procession had passed.

The Wallypug was very thoughtful for some time after the Queen had gone by, and, dur-

THE WALLYPUG LOYALLY WAVED HIS CROWN

ing the drive home, expressed his great surprise that her Majesty had not worn a crown, and apparently could not understand why it should not be worn on all occasions.

"I suppose her Majesty has a crown of her own, hasn't she?" he asked anxiously.

"Oh yes, of course!" I replied.

"Where is it then?" persisted his Majesty.

"I believe all of the regalia is kept carefully locked up and guarded in the Tower of London," I said.

"Well, I think it's very unkind of them not to let her Majesty have them out on an occasion like this. I shall see what I can do about it."

The dear Wallypug's intentions were evidently so good that I did not say anything in reply to this, though I wondered to myself whatever his Majesty thought that *he* could do in the matter.

There were so many people about that we considered it best to spend the rest of the day quietly at home, though we did venture out in the evening to see the illuminations, which delighted his Majesty exceedingly.

The next afternoon the whole party, with

the exception of One-and-Nine, drove over the route taken by the procession, in order to see the street decorations. I remained at home, and late in the afternoon there was a knock at my door, and General Mary Jane entered. She was nervously wringing a handkerchief wet with tears, and her eyes were quite red with weeping.

"Please, sir," she began, sniffing pathetically, "I want to gi—gi—give no—notice."

"Why! what ever for?" I asked in surprise, for General Mary Jane was an excellent servant, and Mrs. Putchy had always been very pleased with her.

"Please, sir, it's Sergeant One-and-Nine; he's broken my 'art, sir, and I can't bear it no longer," and the poor girl burst into a flood of tears.

"Bless me!" I cried, "whatever do you mean?"

"Well, sir, you see ever since he's been 'ere, sir, he's been a making hup to me; leastwise that's what I thought he meant, sir; but this afternoon bein' my day hout, I went up to Kensington Gardens for a walk (him a saying as he would be there), and what should I see when I gets there, but him a walkin' about with half-a-dozen of them nursemaids in white frocks a followin' of him. Not that I says as it's altogether his fault; they will run after the military; but it's more than I can stand, sir, me bein' that proud at 'avin' a soldier for a sweetheart, and all," and she began to cry again.

THEY WILL RUN AFTER THE MILITARY

I hardly knew what to do, but suggested that she should not think too seriously about it, and General Mary Jane, saying she hoped I would excuse her troubling me in the matter, decided to go to her married sister at Barnes and spend the rest of her day out there, and talk the matter over with her. I had a lot of writing to do all the afternoon, and the time passed so quickly that until the gong sounded for dinner I did not realize that the Wallypug and his party had not returned. It was now past seven, and they should have been home hours since.

I was so anxious about them that I could scarcely eat any dinner, and as soon as the meal was over I hurried to the livery stables to hear if they knew anything about the matter.

The first person I encountered when I arrived there was the coachman, now divested of his fine livery, and busy in the yard.

"Bless you, sir, yes, back hours ago," said he. "I set his Majesty and the others down at your door about five o'clock, and I did hear them say something about going down to Hammersmith for a walk."

"To Hammersmith?" I echoed in surprise.

"Yes, sir—they wanted to see the Suspension Bridge and the river again, so I told them the way to get there. They're all right, sir, I'll be bound. The Doctor-in-

Law is too wide awake for anything to happen to them while he is with them."

I walked home somewhat easier in my mind now that I knew the party had returned safely, though still somewhat anxious as to their whereabouts.

About nine o'clock it began to get quite dark, and I was just setting out to see if I could find any trace of them when General Mary Jane returned.

"AND DONKEY RIDES"

"Oh, sir!" she exclaimed directly she saw me, "what do you think? His Majesty and the Doctor-in-Law and the others are down at the fair by Hammersmith Bridge, and they are 'aving such a lark. I see them all 'aving a roundabout as I was coming past on my way 'ome from my sister's just now; such a crowd there was a cheering and a hollering. Cocoa-nut shies, too, a boy told me they had been 'aving, and old Aunt Sally, and donkey rides along the towing path."

"THEY ARE 'AVING SUCH A LARK"

I hurriedly put on my hat and rushed off to Hammersmith, for I didn't know what might happen to my guests among the rough crowd which I knew usually gathered there.

When I arrived on the scene I found the whole party on the roundabout, and when they alighted I learned that the Doctor-in-Law had arranged with one of the show people to share the proceeds of exhibiting the Wallypug and A. Fish, Esq., in separate tents, at 3d. a head.

I met with considerable opposition from the show people in my endeavours to persuade my guests to come home, as they had evidently been a source of considerable profit to them, though the man with the cocoa-nut shies declared that the Doctor-in-Law had claimed a great many more nuts than he was properly entitled to.

The crowd made quite a demonstration when we departed in a four-wheeler, and the Rhymester evidently considered it a compliment that the contents of so many "ladies' tormentors," as the little tubes filled with water are called, were directed at him. Altogether the whole party had evidently been delighted with their evening's amusement, though, as I explained to them while we were driving home, it was highly inconsistent with the dignity of his Majesty's position, and calculated to cause him to be treated with a certain amount of disrespect. I could see, however, that all I said had very little effect on any of the party, and that they were one and all highly delighted with their adventure.

CHAPTER VII

MORE ADVENTURES

"IT'S the most contraryish place I've ever seen," declared One-and-Nine.

"Yes," agreed the Wallypug. "There was no water in the moat."

"The Drawbridge didn't draw," echoed the Rhymester.

"Ad the beefeaters didn't eat beef," chimed in A. Fish, Esq., while the Doctor-in-Law declared that for his part he "considered the morning spent there had been entirely wasted."

They were talking about the Tower of London, and were telling Girlie and Boy, who were spending the afternoon with us, all about their visit there on the previous day.

I was sitting in an adjoining room—but the door being open I could hear all that was said.

"How did you go?" asked Boy.

"Oh!" exclaimed the Wallypug, "in the most extraordinary way you can possibly imagine. We went into a house in High Street, Kensington, and bought some little tickets, and then we handed them to a man at a barrier, who cut a little piece out of each one as we passed through.

"To rebebber us by," chimed in A. Fish, Esq.

"Yes," continued the Wallypug; "and then we went down two flights of stairs, and by-and-bye a lot of little houses on wheels came rushing into the station, and we got into one of them and before you could say 'Jack Robinson' we were rushing through a big black tunnel under the ground."

"Why, you mean the Underground Railway," declared Girlie.

"Yes," agreed his Majesty. "And the little room we sat in had beautiful soft cushions and a big light in the middle of the roof, and little texts printed on the wall—"

"Texts!" exclaimed both of the children.

"Texts," repeated the Wallypug. "What were they? Do you remember?" he asked of the others.

"Oh, one was, 'You are requested not to put your feet on the cushions,'" said the Rhymester.

"Oh, yes, and 'To seat five,' and 'Wait till the train stops'—I remember now," continued the Wallypug. "Well, we kept rushing

"HOLMAN'S MUSTARD AGAIN"

through the tunnel till we came to 'Holman's Mustard,' and a lot of people got out, and then we went on again till we came to 'Smears' Soap.'"

"It wasn't 'Smears' Soap,'" contradicted the Doctor-in-Law. "It was somebody's Ink."

"Well, there were such a lot of names," declared the Wallypug, "it was impossible to really tell which was which. I always took the name opposite to my window to be the right one. The funniest part of it all was, we kept coming to 'Holman's Mustard' over and over again. I can't think how on earth the people know when to get out."

"Why, those weren't the names of the stations at all," laughed Boy. "They were advertisements!"

"Well, where were the names of the stations then?" demanded his Majesty.

"Why, in big letters on the walls of course," was the reply.

"They couldn't have been much bigger than those of 'Holman's Mustard,'" persisted the Wallypug somewhat ungrammatically.

"Never mind about that; get on with your story," remarked the Doctor-in-Law impatiently.

"Well, after going through a lot of tunnels and stopping ever so many times, we got out at one of the stations and went upstairs into the light again, and almost opposite the station we could see a lot of grey stone buildings with towers and battlements."

"I know! You mean the Tower. We've been there," interrupted Girlie.

"Did you see the Lions?" asked the Wallypug eagerly.

"Lions! No!" exclaimed the children. "There weren't any; you didn't see any, did you?"

"No, we didn't," admitted the Wallypug, "but the Doctor-in-Law told us that there were some there."

"I read it in a book," declared the Doctor-in-Law. "But I daresay it was all a pack of stories, like the rest of the things they said. Look at the Crown Jewels for instance—bits of glass and rubbish. That's why they put them in an iron cage, so you can't get at them to see if they are real."

"Oh! I think they *are* real," said Boy. "The Guide told us that they were worth ever so many thousands of pounds."

"Yes, he may have *said* so," remarked the Doctor-in-Law, "but I'll be bound he wouldn't let you take them away and examine them for yourself. I asked them to let me have one or two of the crowns and things to take home and test, but they positively refused, although I promised to return them within a week. They are afraid that we should find out that they are only imitations — that's what's the matter."

"There weren't any kings or queens executed either the day we were there," he continued, grumbling.

"Well, I'm sure I'm very glad that *that* fashion has died out," declared his Majesty. "I don't mind admitting now that I was rather nervous about going at all, for fear that I should have *my* head chopped off, and I should feel so very awkward without one, you know."

"Pooh! You needn't have been alarmed, for there wasn't a Lord High Executioner on the premises, because I asked," declared the Rhymester.

"No, but do you know," said his Majesty, "I've found out since, that he lives at the bottom of our street, and mends shoes for a living—he does a little executing still on the sly, for I have seen his bill in the window, 'Orders *executed* with promptness and dispatch.' I asked him one day what class he executed most, and he said that his connection was principally amongst the 'Uppers.' He seems a very kind man though, and not only executes orders, but heals them too, poor souls! He charges 1s. 3d. for healing. His education has been sorely neglected, I am afraid, however, for he spells it 'heeling.'"

"Did you see the Armoury at the Tower?" asked Boy.

"Yes, and there was another instance of deception," declared the Doctor-in-Law.

"What do you mean?" asked Boy.

"Well, what is an armoury?" inquired the Doctor-in-Law.

"A place where arms are kept, I suppose," replied Boy.

"Just so, and there wasn't an arm in the place except our own," said the Doctor-in-Law wrathfully.

"Why, they call guns and things arms," said Boy, laughing.

"Oh! do they?" remarked the Doctor-in-Law sarcastically. "Why don't they call things by their proper names then? they might as well call them legs, or turnips, or paraffin oil—bah! I've no patience with such folly!"

"I think they bight feed the raveds[1] bedder," complained A. Fish, Esq. "They went for by calves, and if wud of those Beefeaters hadn'd

[1] He meant the tame ravens which are kept at the Tower.

"THEY WENT FOR BY CALVES"

cub and driven theb away I shouldn't have had a leg left to stand up od."

"Beefeaters, yes!" remarked the Rhymester, "and a pretty lot they were. I tried several of them with a piece that I had brought with me in a little paper bag, and not one of them would touch it."

"Madame Tussaud's was better; we went there in the afternoon," said his Majesty.

"Yes, but who was to know which were wax figures and which were not?" asked the Doctor-in-Law.

"Well, you made a pretty muddle of it anyhow," said the Wallypug. "Do you know," he went on, "the Doctor-in-Law made us all pay sixpence each towards the catalogue, and then went around with us explaining the various groups. He had just finished telling us that several ladies, who were standing together, were Henry the Eighth's wives, when they all marched off looking highly indignant."

"Well, how was I to know?" remarked the Doctor-in-Law pettishly. "I'd never met a single one of Henry the Eighth's wives in my life, and how was I to recognize them?"

"I don't think they would have binded so

butch if the Rhymebster hadn't pinched wud of theb to see if they were alive or dot," remarked A. Fish, Esq.

"Did you see the Sleeping Beauty?" asked Girlie.

"Oh, yes! Isn't it cruel to keep her shut up in that case," cried the Wallypug. "I'm

HE COULD GET NO ANSWER

sure she's alive, for we could see her breathing quite distinctly. I was so concerned about it that I asked the Doctor-in-Law to speak to a policeman who was standing near by about it. But he could get no answer from him, and we found out afterwards that he was only a wax figure."

"The best thig of all," remarked A. Fish, Esq., "was whed we all pretended that we—"

"Dear me, it's very warm!" interrupted the Doctor-in-Law. "Let's change the subject."

"Pretended that we—" continued A. Fish, Esq.

"Hush—sh—sh—!" cried the Doctor-in-Law in a warning voice.

"The fact of the matter is," explained the Rhymester, "the Doctor-in-Law got us all to pretend that we were wax figures ourselves, and he tied little money boxes in front of us with the words: 'Put a penny in the slot and the figure will move,' written on them, and when anyone put a penny in we all moved our heads and rolled our eyes about."

"I didn't!" said the Wallypug.

"No, I know you didn't," replied the Rhymester. "And the Doctor-in-Law had to explain that you were out of order, and that's how we were found out, for the people wanted their money back and he wouldn't give it to them, so they called the attendant, and we had to go out as quickly as we could."

"Ad wasn't id beade?" said A. Fish, Esq.

"There were four shillings ad threepedce id the boxes, ad the Doctor-id-Law wouldn't give us a penny of id."

"Well, I let you pay my fare home. That amounted to the same thing," replied the little man.

Just then Mrs. Putchy came in with afternoon tea, and I joined my guests in the drawing-room.

CHAPTER VIII

HIS MAJESTY IS INTERVIEWED

THE next morning we were all seated around the breakfast table laughing over our adventures of the evening before, when we had visited the Earl's Court Exhibition together. We had been up in the Great Wheel, and having passed through the pretty old English village were walking around the artificial lake listening to the band playing in their little pavilion on the island in the middle, when the Doctor-in-Law declared that he heard a strange trumpeting sound, and asked me what it could be. I had not heard it and so could not tell him, and we were just discussing the matter when the Wallypug clutched wildly at his crown, and turning around we saw a huge elephant lifting it gracefully off his head with its trunk.

Directly his Majesty realized what it was, he gave a wild scream and took to his heels, as did all the others, with the exception of the Rhymester, who tripped against a stone and lay with his head buried in his arms for some time, kicking and screaming for help.

Of course it was only the tame elephant that carries the children on its back, but to the unaccustomed eyes of the Wallypug and his party it seemed, so they told me afterwards, some strange and awful monster ready to devour them.

As I said, we were laughing merrily over this adventure when the postman arrived, and the Doctor-in-Law, without asking to be excused from the table, rushed out to meet him, and returned a few minutes later with his arms loaded with a number of little packages and one rather large box, which had arrived by Carter Paterson.

"Dear me, what a lot of letters," remarked his Majesty.

"Yes. Wouldn't you like to know what they are all about, eh?" inquired the Doctor-in-Law.

"Yes, I should," admitted the Wallypug;

A STRANGE AND AWFUL MONSTER

HIS MAJESTY IS INTERVIEWED

while the faces of the others all expressed the same curiosity.

"Well, I'll tell you what I'll do," said the Doctor-in-Law. "If you'll all pay me fourpence halfpenny each, I will let you open them and see for yourselves."

There was a little grumbling at this, but eventually the money changed hands, and, the breakfast things having been removed, the little packages were opened with great eagerness.

Besides a printed circular, each one contained some little article—a pencil case, a pen knife, a comb, a sample tin of knife polish, a card of revolving collar studs, and so on.

"Ah!" remarked the Doctor-in-Law complacently as these articles were spread about the table; "I told you that I expected to derive a princely revenue from my correspondence, and now I will explain to you how it is done. I observed a great number of advertisements in the daily papers, stating that 'A handsome income could be earned without the slightest trouble or inconvenience, and particulars would be forwarded to any one sending six stamps and an addressed envelope';

so I sent off about twenty, and here is the result. I see by these circulars that I have only to sell two hundred of these little pencil cases at half-a-crown each in order to earn 1s. 6d. commission, and for every dozen tins of knife polish I sell, I shall be paid 1½d., besides being able to earn 6d. a thousand by addressing envelopes for one firm, if I supply my own envelopes."

"What's in the big box?" inquired the Rhymester.

"A dittig bachede," replied A. Fish, Esq., who had been busily engaged in opening it.

"A what?" exclaimed the others.

"A dittig bachede for dittig socks," repeated A. Fish, Esq.

"Oh yes, of course!" explained the Doctor-in-Law, "a knitting machine. I was persuaded to buy it on the understanding that I was to have constant work all the year round, and be paid so much per pair for knitting socks with it. It's a most interesting and amusing occupation, and, I'll tell you what, I don't mind letting any one of you use the machine for sixpence an hour, if you find your own worsted and give me the socks when they are finished. There now! nothing could be fairer than that, could it?"

And positively A. Fish, Esq., was so infatuated with the charms of the "dittig

THE "DITTIG BACHEDE"

bachede," as he called it, that he actually agreed to these terms, and sent out for some worsted, and commenced "dittig" with great enthusiasm. The Doctor-in-Law then set the Rhymester to work, addressing the envelopes on the understanding that he was to share the sixpence per thousand to be paid for them. And, having bothered the Wallypug and myself into buying a pencil-case and a knife each, in order to get rid of him, he started off to the kitchen to see if he could do any business with Mrs. Putchy in the knife-polish or black-lead line.

His Majesty and myself were just saying what an extraordinary little man he was, when he burst in upon us again.

"Heard the news?" he inquired, his face beaming with importance.

"No. What is it?" inquired the others eagerly.

"Ah! wouldn't you like to know?" exclaimed the Doctor-in-Law. "How much will you give me for telling you?"

"How much do you want?" asked the Rhymester dubiously.

"A penny each," was the reply.

"Come on then, let's have it," said the Rhymester, collecting the pennies from the others and handing them to the Doctor-in-Law.

"Why—er—er—Queen Anne is dead, and

the Dutch have taken Holland—yah!" And the little man burst out laughing.

"Oh! I say, that's *too* bad," grumbled the Wallypug. "Isn't it now?" he cried, appealing to me.

"Well, really," I replied, "you shouldn't be so silly as to give him money. You ought to know by this time what to expect from him."

"No, but truly," said the Doctor-in-Law, pulling a serious face, "I *have* got some news, the other was only my fun. A lady is going to call on us at eleven, to interview the Wallypug. I had almost forgotten it."

"A lady!" I exclaimed. "Whoever do you mean?"

"Oh, she's the Duchess of something. I forget her name," answered the Doctor-in-Law nonchalantly. "She called the other day while you were out, and explained that she was a contributor to one of the latest society magazines, and was anxious to send an illustrated interview with the Wallypug, to her paper; so—ahem!—after we had come to terms, I arranged for her to come to-day and see him. You had better go and make yourself tidy, hadn't you?" he continued, turning to the Wallypug.

"Well, really," I interposed, "I think you might have consulted his Majesty first, before making these arrangements."

"Oh! do you?" said the Doctor-in-Law rudely. "Well, I don't see that it's any business of yours, my good sir—so there!" and he bounced out of the room again, rattling his sample tins.

It was nearly eleven then, and a few minutes afterwards a beautifully-appointed carriage drew up to the door, and Mrs Putchy brought up a card inscribed:

> Her Grace the Duchess of Mortlake.

and immediately ushered in a fashionably-dressed lady, who smilingly offered me the tips of her fingers.

"Oh, *how* do you do? You are the gentleman, I think, who is to introduce me to his Majesty, are you not?"

"Well, really, your Grace, we have only just heard of the appointment, but his Majesty the Wallypug will be very pleased to receive you I am sure."

HIS MAJESTY IS INTERVIEWED

"And is that his Majesty at the other end of the room?" whispered the Duchess. "Pray present me."

I made the necessary introduction, and the Duchess gave the regulation Court 'dip,' which the Wallypug gravely imitated, and then in his usual simple manner offered his hand with a smile.

IN THE MOST APPROVED FASHION

Her Grace made a deep presentation curtsey and bowed over it in the most approved fashion; but the Wallypug, evidently unused to being treated with so much ceremony, withdrew it hastily and remarked nervously but politely:

"Won't you take a seat, madam?"

"Say, 'Your Grace,'" I whispered.

"What for?" asked his Majesty blankly.

"Because this lady is a Duchess, and you must always say 'Your Grace' when speaking to her," I replied.

"Oh!" said the Wallypug vaguely—then going up to the Duchess he solemnly said, "I'm Grace."

"No, no!" I explained. "You don't understand me. I mean, when you speak to this lady you must call her 'Your Grace.'"

"Dear me, how stupid of me, to be sure!" said his Majesty. "I understand now. I beg your pardon. I meant to say, 'You are my Grace,' madam," he continued, addressing himself to the Duchess.

Her Grace amiably laughed away this little mistake, and was soon busy asking questions. The Wallypug, however, got very nervous, and made a shocking lot of mistakes in his answers. He couldn't even say how old he was.

"I know I've been in the family for years," he remarked, "and I fancy I must have come over with William the Conqueror. Such a lot of people did that, you know, and it's so respectable. I don't remember it, of course;

HIS MAJESTY IS INTERVIEWED

but then I've been told that I was born very young, and so naturally I shouldn't do so."

"Does your Majesty remember any of the incidents of your early life?" asked the Duchess.

"I was considered remarkably bald for my age as an infant," replied the Wallypug simply. "And I believe I had several measles, and a mump or two as a child. But I don't wish to boast about them," he added modestly.

"Where were you educated, your Majesty?" was the next question.

"I wasn't," replied the Wallypug with a sigh.

"Does your Majesty mean that you received no education at all?" asked the Duchess in surprise.

"Oh! I was taught reading, and writing, and arithmetic, and the use of the globes, and Latin and Greek, and all that rubbish, of course," replied the Wallypug. "But I mean there were no Universities at Why, where I could receive a higher education, and be taught cricket, and football, and rowing, and all those classical things taught at Oxford and Cambridge, you know. I was considered the best boy in my form at marbles though," he added proudly. "And I could beat any of the masters at Hop Scotch."

"What is your favourite diet, your Majesty?" came next.

"Oh! jumbles, I think—or bull's eyes. I'm very fond of hardbake too, and I love cocoanut ice."

A few more questions such as these, and her Grace took her departure, after taking several snap-shot photographs of various articles in the drawing room.

I felt convinced that with such a scanty amount of information at her disposal the Duchess would have great difficulty in writing an article on the Wallypug, and was therefore the more surprised a few days later to receive a copy of the magazine which her Grace represented, with a long and particular account of the interview, under the heading of, "'Why Wallypug and wherefore of Why?' by a Lady of Title." Into it her Grace had introduced the most preposterous and extravagant statements about his Majesty.

We learned with amazement that "The Wallypug came of a very ancient family, and had early been distinguished for many remarkable accomplishments. While at school his Majesty displayed such a natural aptitude for learning as to readily out-distance his instructors."

"I suppose that's because I said I played Hop Scotch better than the masters," commented his Majesty, to whom I was reading the account aloud.

Photographs of various articles in the drawing-room, which had no connection whatever with the Wallypug, were reproduced with the most extraordinary and absolutely untrue stories attached to them.

THE FAITHFUL HOUND

Dick and Mrs. Mehetable Murchison appeared as "The Wallypug's favourite cat and dog," while pathetic stories were told of how the dog had on several occasions saved his royal master from an untimely and watery grave, while the cat had prevented him from being burned to death while reading in bed by gently scratching his nose when he had fallen asleep, and the candle had set fire to the bed curtains. Sensational illustrations were also given depicting these incidents, which of course were purely imaginary.

It was very remarkable to notice though, that directly the article of the Duchess's appeared, invitations from all sorts of grand people poured in upon us—and the daily papers suddenly woke up to the fact that the

THE SAGACIOUS PUSSY

Wallypug and his suite were very important personages, and devoted whole columns to "Our Mysterious Foreign Guests," as they called them.

There was always more or less of a crowd outside the house now, and when his Majesty drove in the Park, the people all stood up on the little green seats to get a better view of him as he passed.

CHAPTER IX

THE WALLYPUG'S OWN

IT was shortly after this that the Doctor-in-Law, hearing what a vast fortune might be made in literature, decided to start a magazine of his own.

THE DOCTOR-IN-LAW WAS EDITOR

After a lot of argument it was thought best to call it *The Wallypug's Own*, as the name was considered a striking one. The first number was to be a very elaborate affair, and, for weeks before it appeared, all of my guests were busily engaged in its production.

"There will be a good opportunity for some of your poems appearing at last," hinted the Doctor-in-Law to the Rhymester, which so delighted the poor little fellow that he set to work at once upon a number of new ones. A. Fish, Esq., contributed a very learned article on the subject of "The Prevalence of Toothache amongst Fish: its Cause and Treatment"; while the great attraction of the number was an historical article by the Wallypug on the subject of "Julius Caesar," illustrated by his Majesty himself. As a special favour, the original drawing was presented to me by his Majesty, and I am thus enabled to reproduce it for your benefit. His Majesty confided to me that parts of it were traced from a picture which appeared in the *Boys' Own Paper* some time ago, but of course we did not tell everybody that.

The essay itself was quite original, and was worded somehow like this:

"*Julius Caesar was a man, and he lived in Rome. He came over to conquer Britain because he heard* there was a lot of tin here, and when he arrived he said in Latin, 'Veni, vidi, vici,' which means, 'I have come, and thou wilt have to skedaddle,' which has been the British motto ever since. But the Ancient Britons who lived here then, didn't understand Latin, and so they went for Julius Caesar, and shook their fists in his face, and tried to drive him

FROM "THE WALLYPUG'S OWN"

and his followers away. But Julius Caesar and the Romans were civilized, and had daggers and things, and shields, and wore firemen's helmets, aud kilts like Scotchmen, so they soon overcame the Ancient Britons; and they built London Wall, and made a lot of combs, and glass tear-bottles, and brooches, and sarcophaguses, that you can see in the Museum at the Guildhall; and then they went back to Rome, and Julius Caesar was stabbed by his friend Brutus, *to show how much he liked him; and Caesar, when he found out he was stabbed, cried out in Latin, 'Et tu, Brute,' which means 'Oh, you brute,' and lived happy ever after. I have drawn the picture of Julius Caesar landing in Britain—that's him waving things, and calling to the others to come on."*

The Doctor-in-Law was editor, and arranged a number of competitions, and in order to enter for them you had only to send two shillings in stamps, while the prizes were advertised as follows: First prize, £1000 a year for life; second prize, thirty-six grand pianos and fourteen bicycles; third prize, a sewing machine and six cakes of scented soap. The prizes were to be awarded for the first correct answers received by post, but the Doctor-in-Law took good care to write three sets of answers himself, and put them in our letter-box a half-an-hour before the first post arrived, so that nobody got prizes but himself. He made a good deal of money, too, by pretending to tell your fortune by the creases in your collar. All you had to do was to send an old collar and fourteen penny stamps, and you would receive a letter in reply similar to this:

"You are probably either a male or a female,

and will no doubt live till you die. You like to have your own way when you can get it, and when you can't you get very cross and irritable. You are not so young as you were a few years ago, and you dislike pain of any kind. You will remain single until you marry, and whichever you do you will probably wish you hadn't."

The greatest novelty, however, which the Doctor-in-Law introduced in his new magazine was his system of telling your character by your watch and chain. There was no fee charged, and all you had to do was to send your watch and chain (gold preferred), and the Doctor-in-Law would tell your character, quite correctly. It generally was as follows:

"You are a silly donkey, for no one but a donkey would think of sending his watch and chain to a stranger, and if you imagine that you will ever see it again, you are greatly mistaken."

The Rhymester only had one poem in after all, as, when it came to the point, the Doctor-in-Law charged him a guinea a verse for printing it, and the poor Rhymester could not afford more than one poem at that rate.

THE NEW ROBIN.

The North wind doth blow,
And we ought to have snow,
If 'tis true what my nurse used to sing,
      Poor thing.

Yet up in yon tree
Robin Redbreast I see
As happy and gay as a king,
      Poor thing.

Look! as true as I live,
There's a boy with a sieve
And a stick and a long piece of string,
      Poor thing.

But the bird doesn't care,
For I hear him declare,
"Pooh! the old dodge he tried in the Spring,
      Poor thing."

"What ridiculous cheek,"
And he turns up his beak
Ere he tucks his head under his wing,
      Poor thing.

The poor Rhymester was very disappointed at not being able to publish more of his poems, so the Doctor-in-Law, to console him, allowed him to contribute an article on " Fashions for the Month by Our Paris Model." He made a frightful muddle of it though, not knowing the proper terms in which to describe the various materials and styles. Here is an extract, which will show you better than I can tell, the stupid blunders which he made:

"*Hats this season are principally worn on the head, and may be trimmed with light gauzy stuff wobbled round the crown mixed up with various coloured ribbons, and bunches of artificial flowers and fruit.*

"*Artificial vegetables are not much worn, although a cauliflower or two and a bunch of carrots, with a few cabbages, would form a striking and novel decoration for a hat. If this trimming is considered insufficient, a few brightly coloured tomatoes stuck round the brim might be added, and would render the head-gear particularly 'chic.'*

"*Hats for the theatre should be worn large and handsomely trimmed, but for the economically inclined—a last year's clothes basket trimmed with art muslin, which may be purchased of any good draper at $1\frac{3}{4}d$. a yard, cut on the cross and tucked with chiffons, would form a sweetly simple hat, and if tied beneath the chin with an aigrette, and the front filled in with sequins, it would readily be mistaken for one of the new early Victorian bonnets which continue to be worn by the upper housemaids in most aristocratic families.*

"*I hear that dresses are to be worn again this year by ladies. The most fashionable ones will be made of various sorts of material.*

"*A charming walking costume suitable for the Autumn may be made of shaded grenadine, trimmed with buckram pom-poms, made up on the selvedge edge.*"

There was a lot more nonsense of this kind which I did not at all understand, but which some lady friends who understood these things made great fun of.

You will be surprised, no doubt, to hear that in a weak moment I allowed myself to be persuaded into contributing a little experience of my own.

The Rhymester told me that it was shockingly bad rhyme, but I think that he was jealous because the Doctor-in-Law published it. Anyhow, here it is, so you can judge for yourself. I call it

HE AND I AND IT.

Oh HE was a Publisher
And I was a Publishee,
   And IT was a book
   Which the Publisher took
And pub-l-i-s-h-e-d.

The Publisher's smile it was bland,
'Twas a beautiful smile to see,
   As again and again
   He took pains to explain
How large my "half-profits" *might* be.

IT had a capital sale,
Well reviewed by the *Times* and *D.T.*,
   And a great many more,
   So my friends by the score
Came around to congratulate me.

IT HAD A CAPITAL SALE

And people I scarcely had met,
Just "dropped in" to afternoon tea;
   While my aunt, who's a swell,
   Now remembered quite well
That I was related to she.

And girls that were rich and plain,
Or pretty and poor, did agree
   To let me suppose
   That I'd but to propose
To be m-a-r-r-i-e-d.

MY FRIENDS ALL TURNED TAIL

Yes, HE published IT in the Spring,
That season of frolic and glee;
   "In the Autumn," HE said,
   Gravely nodding his head,
"'Half-profits' will mean L.S.D."

But Autumn has come and gone,
And I'm so to say, "All at sea,"
   For HE sobs and HE sighs
   And HE turns up his eyes
When I ask what my "half-profits" be.

There are "charges for this, and for that,"
And for "things that HE couldn't foresee,"
  And HE "very much fears,"
  So he says twixt his tears,
"That there won't be a penny for me."

Oh! rich is the Publisher
And poor is the Publishee;
  Of the profits of IT
  I shall touch not a bit,
They are all swallowed up by HE.

The girls now all treat me with scorn—
Aunt turns up her n-o-s-e,
  And my friends all turn tail,
  While my book they assail
And call rubbish and twad-d-l-e.

Even One-and-Nine and General Mary Jane were smitten with a desire to rush into print, and I overheard them concocting a tragic Love Story in the kitchen, and they were highly indignant later on, because the Doctor-in-Law would not accept it. You can hardly wonder at it though, for it really was too bad for anything.

It was called "The Viscount's Revenge," and in it several characters who had been killed in the first part of the book kept cropping up all through the story in a most confusing manner, while One-and-Nine and

General Mary Jane could not agree as to whether the heroine should be dark or fair, so in one part of the book she had beautiful

THE LITERARY HOUSEMAID

golden hair and blue eyes, and in another she was described as "darkly, proudly handsome, with a wealth of dusky hair and eyes as black as night."

At the last moment it was found necessary to include another poem in the magazine, and, as all of the Rhymester's were too long, the Doctor-in-Law decided to write one himself, which he called

COMMERCIAL PROBLEMS.

Why doth the little busy bee
    Not charge so much an hour,
For gathering honey day by day
    From every opening flower?

And can you tell me why, good sir,
    The birds receive no pay
For singing sweetly in the grove
    Throughout the livelong day?

Why flow'rs should bloom about the place
    And give their perfume free,
In so unbusinesslike a way,
    Seems very odd to me.

I cannot meet a single cow
    That charges for her milk,
And though they are not paid a sou,
    The silkworms still spin silk.

While ducks and hens, I grieve to find,
    Lay eggs for nothing too,
Which is a most ridiculous
    And foolish thing to do.

These problems often puzzle me;
  I lie awake at night,
And think and think what I can do
  To set this matter right.

I've found a way at last, and though
  It may at first seem funny,
It cannot fail—'tis this : *You* pay,
  And *I'll* collect the money.

CHAPTER X

THE WALLYPUG GOES TO WINDSOR

WHILE they were all busy in the preparation of *The Wallypug's Own*, I thought it an excellent opportunity to run down to Folkestone in order to make arrangements for hiring a house, as I intended taking my guests to the seaside for a few weeks.

I felt a little anxious about leaving them to themselves, but hoped that they would be too busy and interested in the new magazine to get into trouble.

It was most unfortunate that I should have gone just then though, for directly I had left the Wallypug received a polite letter from one of the Court officials to say that the Queen would be pleased to receive his Majesty and suite at Windsor on the following day.

Of course, as you may imagine, the Wallypug was in a great state of excitement at receiving this royal invitation, and wished to telegraph at once for me to return and advise them how to act and what to do, on this important occasion; however, the Doctor-in-Law,

A ROYAL INVITATION

so I have been given to understand, persuaded his Majesty not to do anything of the sort, and added that I "was always poking about and interfering, and was better out of the way"; so his Majesty, who was very anxious to do the right thing, consulted Mrs. Putchy as to the proper costume to be worn, and the etiquette to be observed.

"Well, your Majesty," remarked Mrs. Putchy in reply, "I scarcely know what to advise. When in my younger days, I acted as lady's maid to the Countess of Wembley, I know her ladyship wore a Court train and carried a bouquet when she was presented to the Queen."

"Where did the engine go?" asked his Majesty curiously.

"The engine!" exclaimed Mrs. Putchy.

"Yes; you said she wore a train, didn't you?" said the Wallypug.

"Oh! but I didn't mean that kind of train," laughed Mrs. Putchy; "I meant a long sort of cloak fastened on to the shoulders and trailing along the ground at the back—they are generally made of satin and velvet, and are decorated with flowers and feathers and lace, and that sort of thing. Your Majesty's cloak would do nicely if I trimmed it for you."

"But are you sure that gentlemen wear these sort of things?" inquired the Wallypug.

"Well, I couldn't rightly say, your Majesty, but I'm sure I've seen pictures of kings and such like wearing trains which were borne by pages, so I feel sure your Majesty would be safe in wearing one."

So it was arranged that, after having been carefully brushed, his Majesty's velvet cloak was to be gaily decorated with lace and large bunches of flowers, and, to make the thing complete, a large bouquet was tied around his sceptre, and, at the Rhymester's suggestion, little knots of flowers were attached to the knobs of his Majesty's crown.

The little man was highly delighted with his appearance when all these arrangements were concluded, and could get but very little sleep that night for thinking of the great honour which was to be his the next day.

The whole household was early astir in the morning, and at about eleven o'clock the carriage came to take the royal guests to the station.

Arrived at Waterloo, the Doctor-in-Law, after making various inquiries as to the price of the tickets, etc., actually had the meanness, despite the remonstrance of the railway officials, to insist upon the whole party travelling down third-class, remarking that he "found the third-class carriages reached there quite as soon as the first, and a penny saved was a penny gained."

The station master at Windsor was particularly put out about it, as, in honour of his Majesty's visit, the station had been gaily decorated and a carpet laid down to the carriage door. His Majesty, however, made a brave show as he walked up the platform preceded by the Doctor-in-Law, his gaily decorated train borne by the Rhymester, and followed by A. Fish, Esq., and One-and-Nine, the latter carrying a mysterious bandbox, which contained a present from the Wallypug to her Majesty. (See frontispiece.)

Inside and out the station was crowded with curious spectators, all eager to catch a glimpse of his Majesty and his remarkable retinue, and cheer after cheer resounded as the station master, bare-headed and bowing, ushered the party to the royal carriage with the red and gold-liveried servants, which had been sent from the castle to meet them.

The bells were ringing, and the streets were crowded as they drove through the old town, and his Majesty thoroughly enjoyed the drive, while the Doctor-in-Law was quite in his element amidst all this fuss and excitement.

I did not care to inquire too fully into the details of his Majesty's interview with the Queen, but I was given to understand that the whole party was treated with the utmost kindness.

Her Majesty graciously accepted at the Wallypug's hands a gilded crown, an exact copy of the one he wore himself, and which he had had made expressly for her Majesty, having been struck by the fact that her Majesty's real crown was always kept locked up in the Tower, and hoping that perhaps this one would do for second best.

I could not gather that her Majesty had actually promised to wear it, but I do know that the Wallypug was made exceedingly proud and happy by the gift of a portrait of her Majesty herself, with the royal autograph attached, and that he will always remember the occasion of his visit to Windsor, and the kindness with which he was treated by everyone, particularly by the little Princes and Princesses, her Majesty's great grand-children, who led him about the Castle grounds, and showed him their pets, and the flowers, and conservatories, and all the wonderful sights of that wonderful place.

In the evening there was a dinner party, at which her Majesty did not appear, and early the next morning a royal carriage again drove them to the station *en route* for London.

All this I learned on my return from Folkestone. I also heard of an extraordinary evening party which had been given at my house during my absence. It appears that the invitations had been sent out by the Doctor-in-Law the very day upon which I left, and about thirty guests, including the Duchess of Mortlake, had been invited. Unfortunately, however, this visit to Windsor had entirely driven the matter from the Wallypug's mind, and the others had forgotten about it too, and so a pretty confusion was the result.

It appears that one evening about seven o'clock they were all in the kitchen making toffee, having persuaded Mrs. Putchy to let them have the frying-pan and some sugar and butter, and it having been cooking for some time the Doctor-in-Law had just told the Wallypug to stick his finger in and see if it was done, when Mrs. Putchy came in to say that some ladies and gentlemen had arrived, and were waiting in the drawing-room.

TO SEE IF IT WAS DONE

All of a sudden it flashed upon their minds that *this* was the evening upon which they had invited their visitors to the party. Whatever was to be done? Not the slightest preparation had been made—and his Majesty and the others were all more or less in a sticky condition, and quite unfit to be seen by company.

A hurried consultation took place, during which they could hear more and more guests arriving, and at last, by a brilliant inspiration, the Doctor-in-Law thought of making it a surprise party, similar to those given in America.

"It won't cost us anything either," he remarked complacently.

"But what is a surprise party?" asked the others.

"Never mind, you'll see presently," remarked the little man. "Run and wash your hands now and make yourselves tidy."

A few minutes later the whole party filed into the drawing-room, the Wallypug looking rather blank and nervous, and the Doctor-in-Law full of profuse apologies for having kept the guests waiting so long.

"By the way," he remarked airily, "I suppose you all know that it's a surprise party."

"Dear me, no," said the Duchess of Mortlake, speaking for the others. "Whatever is that; I don't think it was mentioned on the cards of invitation, was it?"

"Ah! a trifling oversight," remarked the Doctor-in-Law. "A surprise party," he continued in explanation, "is one at which each guest is expected to contribute something towards the supper—some bring one thing and some another. What have you brought, may I ask, your Grace?"

"Well, really," said the Duchess, "I've never heard of such a thing in my life before. I've not brought anything at all, of course; I'm surprised at your asking me such a question."

"Ah, yes, just so," remarked the Doctor-in-Law triumphantly, "just what I told you—a *surprise* party, don't you see! Now, what I would advise is that you should all go out and order various things to be sent in for supper; we, for our part, will provide some excellent toffee, and then you can come back and help us to set the tables and all that sort of thing, you know—it's the greatest fun in the world, I assure you."

And really the little man carried it off with such gaiety, that entering into the spirit of the thing the guests really did as he suggested, and went out and ordered the things, and afterwards came back, and, amidst great laughter and fun, the tables were laid, every one doing some share of the work, with the exception of the Doctor-in-Law, who contented himself with directing the others and chatting to the ladies.

The poor dear Wallypug amiably toiled backward and forward between the kitchen and dining-room with great piles of plates and other heavy articles, and A. Fish, Esq., in his eagerness to help, was continually treading on his

THE WALLYPUG HELPS

own tail, upsetting himself and the various dishes entrusted to his charge.

At last, however, the supper was set, and the merriest evening you can possibly imagine was spent by the guests. His Majesty was in capital spirits, and after supper suggested a little dancing, which suggestion was hailed with delight by the others, and, having moved some of the furniture out of the drawing-room and pushed the rest away into corners, the Wallypug led off with her Grace the Duchess of Mortlake, and quite distinguished himself

A. FISH, ESQ., UPSET

in "Sir Roger de Coverley." Afterwards there was a little singing and music, several of the guests contributing to the evening's entertainment. Amongst other items was a song by A. Fish, Esq., rendered as well as his bad cold would permit, of which the first lines ran:

I'b siddig here ad lookig at the bood, love,
  Ad thinkig ov the habby days of old,
Wed you ad I had each a wooded spood, love,
  To eat our porridge wed we had a cold.

Altogether the evening was such a success that her Grace declared that it should not be her fault if surprise parties were not the fashion in Society during the coming winter.

CHAPTER XI

HIS MAJESTY AT THE SEASIDE

I SENT Mrs. Putchy and General Mary Jane down to the house, which I had engaged on the "Lees" at Folkestone, the day before we were to go, in order to see that everything was ready for us.

"The only thing that is wrong is the kitchen chimney, and that smokes, sir," said Mrs. Putchy, in answer to my inquiry on the night of our arrival. "I think that we had better have the sweep in the morning, sir."

"Very well, Mrs. Putchy, I'm sure you know best," I replied, and thought no more of the matter.

Early in the morning, however, I was awakened by screams and cries proceeding from the lower part of the house.

"Help! help! Burglars! Fire and police!

Thieves!" screamed a voice, and hastily dressing myself, I rushed out into the passage, and was confronted by the Rhymester, who had evidently just jumped out of bed, and who, though it was broad daylight, bore a lighted candle in one hand, and a pair of fire tongs in the other.

His teeth were chattering with fright, and his knees were knocking together from the same cause.

"What's the matter," I asked in alarm.

"Oh! oh! there are burglars in the house," he cried excitedly, "and the others have gone down to them; I'm sure they'll be killed—I told them not to go, but they would. Let's go and hide under a bed somewhere. Oh! oh, what will become of us?"

"Don't be such a coward," I cried, hurrying down stairs, while the poor little Rhymester, afraid to be left alone upstairs, tremblingly followed.

Sure enough there was a sound of struggling going on, and voices raised in loud dispute.

"Oh, that story won't do for me," I heard the Doctor-in-Law exclaim.

"But I tell yez, sor," chimed in another strange voice, "I waz only going to——"

"Never mind what you were going to do, give up the sack," said the Doctor-in-Law.

Then there were sounds of struggling, and amidst the confusion a voice saying:

"Hold him down! Sit on him! That's right! Now for the sack."

And, bursting the door open, a curious sight met my eyes. A poor sweep lay flat upon the floor, with the Wallypug sitting upon him, and One-and-Nine keeping guard; while the Doctor-in-Law and A. Fish, Esq., examined his bag of soot in the corner. The poor little Rhymester summoned up sufficient courage to peep in at the doorway, and stood there making a piteous picture, with his white face and trembling limbs.

"Whatever is the matter," I inquired as soon as I entered.

"We've caught him!" exclaimed his Majesty, complacently wriggling his toes about.

"But what's he been doing," I asked.

"Av ye plaze, sor," groaned the man, panting beneath the Wallypug's weight, "I have been doing nothing at all, at all. I waz just

"WE'VE CAUGHT HIM!"

a-finishin' me warrak of swapin' the chimneys, wen one ov the ould gintleman came up an' poked me in the nose with a sthick, and the other ould gintleman knocked me over and sthole me bag, while the soger hild me down till the other gintleman sat on me—it's among a lot of murtherin' thaves I've got entoirely, savin' yer presince, sor."

"The man is a burglar," declared the Doctor-in-Law emphatically. "I happened to hear a very suspicious noise down here, and calling to the others, rushed down just in time to catch this man making off with a bag of things. I think he was trying to escape up the chimney, for his head was half-way up when we entered, and this bag, which evidently contains plunder of some kind, is covered with soot too."

"Why, the man is a sweep, and was sweeping the chimney," I cried, pointing to his brushes and sticks; and after a lot of explanations the man was told to get up and his Majesty, followed by the others, retired to his bedroom, evidently greatly disappointed that it was not a real burglar that they had been combating.

The sweep, who was a very good-natured Irishman, took it in very good part, and the present of half-a-crown sent him away quite reconciled to his assailants.

The Rhymester afterwards made a great boast that he had not taken any part in the mêlée.

"Of course I knew all along that he wasn't a burglar," he declared, "and that's the reason why I wouldn't interfere."

"You managed to do a good deal of screaming though, I noticed," remarked the Doctor-in-Law grumpily.

"Ah! that was only for fun," asserted the Rhymester.

This was really about the only remarkable incident which occurred during our holiday at Folkestone, which passed very pleasantly and very quietly. We went for a sea bathe nearly every day, and his Majesty would insist upon wearing his crown in the water on every occasion.

"No one will know that I am a king if I don't," he declared; and I am bound to admit that his Majesty did not look very regal in his bathing costume, particularly when he was dripping with water and his long straight hair hung half over his face, and even when he

HIS MAJESTY AT THE SEASIDE 159

wore his crown he was continually catching bits of seaweed in it, which gave him a singularly untidy appearance for a king.

HIS MAJESTY DID NOT LOOK VERY REGAL

A. Fish, Esq., with the assistance of a lifebuoy, nearly learned to swim while we were down there; but the Doctor-in-Law thought that hiring bathing machines was a foolish waste of money, and contented himself with taking off his shoes and stockings and paddling, which he could do without having to pay. One day, however, he was knocked completely over by an incoming wave, and got wet to the skin.

We could never persuade the Rhymester either, to go out further than just to his knees; but I rather fancy that that was because he was afraid of wetting his bathing costume, of which he was particularly proud, and which was decorated with smart little bows of ribbon wherever they could be conveniently put.

Fear may have had something to do with it though, for I noticed that he always clung very tightly to the rope, and never by any chance went beyond its length.

The switchback railway was a source of infinite amusement, and a great deal of time was spent on it. Boating was not much indulged in, as it made one or two of the party, particularly A. Fish, Esq., very ill; but we all enjoyed the beautiful drives in the neighbourhood. There was an excellent Punch and Judy show in the town too, which so

HIS MAJESTY AT THE SEASIDE 161

fascinated his Majesty that we could scarcely tear him away whenever he joined the admiring crowd which daily surrounded it.

The fickle One-and-Nine, while we were here, fell in love with a wax figure exhibited in a hair-dresser's window in Sandgate Road. It represented a beautiful lady with her hair dressed in the latest fashion, and the wooden soldier was greatly infatuated. He spent hours gazing through the window, watching the lady slowly revolve by clockwork; and he became frightfully jealous of the hair-dresser, whom he caught one morning rearranging the drapery around the lady's shoulders.

Eventually, with the assistance of the Rhymester, he composed the following piece of poetry—which he stuck, by means of six gelatine sweets, on to the hair-dresser's window with the writing inside, in order that the lady might see it.

TO THE BEAUTIFUL LADY IN THE HAIR-
DRESSER'S WINDOW.

> I love you, oh! I love you,
>   And I beg you to be mine;
> I'm a gallant wooden soldier,
>   And my name is 1/9.

If you will only marry me,
  'Twill be the greatest fun
To puzzle folks by telling them,
  That we're both 2/1.

'Twill be the truth, for man and wife
  Are one, I beg to state,
This fact's as clear as 4/4,
  Or 2/6 make 8.

They tell me, dear, you have no feet;
  But what is that to me?
2 feet be 4/2 behind
  On animals you see.

That you have none, is o to me,
  Dear 1/4 your sake,
No trifles such as these shall e'er
  My true affections shake.

I bought some penny tarts for you,
  But I am much distrest
To tell you by mistake I sat
  On 1/8 the rest.

One-and-Nine was quite happy in finding that the paper had disappeared from the shop window when he passed by a little later, and declared that it must mean that the lady had accepted him and his poetry.

I think the funniest incident of all though, in connection with our visit to Folkestone, was when his Majesty and the others went into Carlo Maestrani's for some ices.

HIS MAJESTY AT THE SEASIDE 163

They had never tasted any before, and were very much surprised to find them so cold. I shall never forget the expression on the Wallypug's face when, having rather greedily taken a very large mouthful, he could not swallow it, or dispose of it in any way. A. Fish, Esq., declared that it gave him a violent toothache; while the Doctor-in-Law called for the waiter, and insisted upon him taking it away.

"IT'S NOT PROPERLY COOKED"

"It's not properly cooked," he declared angrily, "It's cold."

"Cook, sare, no, sare, it is not cook," agreed the waiter.

"Very well, then, take it away and bring

us some that is. Have it warmed up; do something with it. It's disgraceful bringing us stuff like that."

And no argument or persuasion would convince the little man that the ices were as they should be.

CHAPTER XII

THE DEPARTURE

WE remained at Folkestone till the latter part of September, and then returned to London just about the time that the first number of *The Wallypug's Own* made its appearance.

It caused quite a sensation in literary circles, and was mentioned by most of the papers; but it did *not* turn out a monetary success, and so the Doctor-in-Law declared that he must devise some other means of making money.

We had been once or twice to the circus, and I fancy that it must have been his intention to start something of the sort himself, for I caught him one day trying to teach his Majesty to walk the tight-rope; but as he had only tied the rope between two very light chairs the result was not very satisfactory, particularly to the poor Wallypug, who came to the ground with a terrific crash.

A. Fish, Esq., dressed as a clown, and certainly looked very funny; but his bad cold prevented him from speaking his jokes distinctly, and so the idea was given up.

THE RESULT WAS NOT SATISFACTORY

In fact it was not till November that the Doctor-in-Law hit upon a plan which seemed to give him any great satisfaction. We had been talking a great deal about Guy Fawkes' day and the fireworks at the Crystal Palace, which we intended going to see in the evening.

THE DEPARTURE

and the Doctor-in-Law had been particularly curious to know all about the day and its customs. He did not say much about his plans, but I felt sure that he was up to some of his tricks, for I caught him several times whispering mysteriously to the Rhymester and A. Fish, Esq., and I noticed that they were all particularly kind and respectful to his Majesty, as though they wished to keep him in a good humour.

On the morning of the fifth, when I came down to breakfast, I was greatly surprised to find that the whole party had gone out about an hour previous, after borrowing from Mrs. Putchy a kitchen chair, four broomsticks, and a long piece of clothes-line. Whatever were they up to?

I asked Mrs. Putchy if they had left any message, but no—they had said nothing as to where they were going, what they were going to do, or when they would be back; and the only thing that had struck Mrs. Putchy as being at all remarkable about their appearance, was the fact that the Rhymester had added little bows of coloured ribbon to his costume, and wore a tall pointed cap gaily decorated with streamers, and a deep white frill around his neck—the others were dressed as usual.

I felt sure that some mischief was brewing, and could not settle down to my work for thinking of them. About eleven o'clock I went out to see if I could find any traces of my guests. I had been walking about unsuccessfully for about an hour, when I heard some boys shouting, and turning to look in their direction, I beheld his Majesty calmly seated in a chair which, by means of long poles attached to it, was being carried along by the Rhymester and A. Fish, Esq.

They were followed by a crowd of people who were cheering lustily, and the Doctor-in-Law was rushing about collecting money in his hat, and entreating the people "not to forget the fifth of November," and repeating some doggerel verse about:

> "Guy Fawkes guy,
>   Stick him up high;
> Stick him on a lamp-post,
>   And there let him die,"

while several little boys were dancing about in great excitement, and shouting, "Holler, boys! holler! here's another guy."

A TRIUMPHAL PROCESSION

His Majesty evidently regarded it as a great compliment to himself, and complacently bowed right and left with considerable dignity. And I found out that the Doctor-in-Law had persuaded him into believing that this triumphal procession had been arranged solely in his Majesty's honour.

I was naturally very vexed at the poor Wallypug being imposed upon in this manner, and spoke very plainly to the Doctor-in-Law about it on our way home, and I think the little man must have taken it very much to heart, for he seemed quite subdued, and actually himself suggested sharing the proceeds of the collection with the others.

We went to see the fireworks in the evening, and I don't ever remember seeing the party in such excellent spirits as they were that night.

Mrs. Putchy had prepared a capital supper for us on our return, and I love to remember my friends as they appeared sitting around the supper table talking over the adventures and excitements of the day. I can see them now whenever I close my eyes—the dear old Wallypug at the head of the table, with One-

and-Nine in attendance, and the others all talking at once about the jolly time they had had at the Skating Rink in the afternoon, when A. Fish, Esq., had vainly tried to get along with roller-skates fastened on to his tail.

A CAPITAL STORY

I say I love to remember them thus, for it was the last occasion upon which we were all together. Early the next morning Mrs. Putchy came to my room, and in a very agitated voice said, "Please sir, I'm afraid that there is something wrong; I have knocked at his Majesty's door and can get no answer, and the Doctor-in-Law's room is empty too."

I hurried down, and on the breakfast table

I found a letter addressed to me, in which his Majesty, on behalf of the others, thanked me very heartily for my hospitality, and explained that State matters of the utmost importance had necessitated their immediate return to Why. How they went I have never been able to discover.

The outer door of my flat was found to be locked on the inside as usual, and the windows were all fastened; besides which, as they were some distance from the ground, the Royal party could scarcely have got out that way.

Altogether the whole affair was involved in a mystery which I have never been able to solve to this day. Of course I miss my strange, but withal lovable visitors, very much, and I value very highly the several little mementoes of their visit which remained behind. Amongst others is a cheque of the Doctor-in-Law's for a considerable amount; which, however, I shall never be able to cash, as it is drawn upon the bank of, "Don't-you-wish-you-may-get-it," at Why.

General Mary Jane was inconsolable for some time after the departure of her soldier hero, but eventually married our milkman, a very steady and respectable man in the neighbourhood. Girlie and Boy and many other friends of the Wallypug greatly regretted that they were unable to say good-bye to his Majesty before he left; and often and often, as I sit alone in my study, I think about the simple-natured, good-hearted little fellow, and his remarkable followers, and wonder if I shall ever see them again. Who knows?

I OFTEN THINK OF THEM

THE END

www.ingramcontent.com/pod-product-compliance
Lightning Source LLC
Chambersburg PA
CBHW020245170426
43202CB00008B/238